I0136112

GOD AND EXISTENTIALISM

The Chronicles of a Survivalist

Ben Wood Johnson, Ph.D.

TESKO

Middletown, Pennsylvania

Copyright © 2021 Tesko Publishing Paperback Edition

Copyright © 2018 by Ben Wood Johnson

All rights reserved. No part of this publication may be reproduced, distributed, or transmitted in any form or by any means, including photocopying, recording, or other electronic or mechanical methods, or by any information storage and retrieval system without the prior written permission of the publisher, except in the case of very brief quotations embodied in critical reviews and certain other noncommercial uses permitted by copyright law.

Johnson, Ben Wood

God and Existentialism: The Chronicles of a Survivalist / Ben Wood Johnson.—Tesko Publishing ed.

ISBN-13: 978-1-948600-35-4 (pbk.)

ISBN-10: 1-948600-35-8

The information illustrated in this book was compiled for a school project. The analysis is based on class notes and other materials.

Johnson, Ben Wood

God and Existentialism: The Chronicles of a Survivalist

Tesko Publishing website address: www.teskopublishing.com

Tesko Publishing/Eduka Solutions

330 W. Main St., #214
Middletown, PA 17057, USA

Printed in the United States of America

Cover Illustration Wood Oliver

In memory of my grandmother

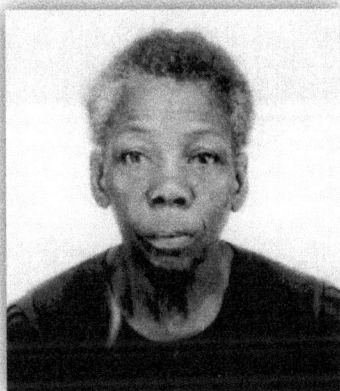

Yvette Vital (Vetto)

Table of Contents

PART III

Growing up among Believers

PART IV

Life if Right Now

Introduction

EXISTENTIALIST PHILOSOPHY claims that men are free. They have free will. They enjoy an uncompromising state of liberty in nature. In earnest, could we say that this is the case?

The previous understandings presume that men are the overseers of their own destiny. What if it were true? What if men were—indeed—in charge of their own existence? What would that reality implicate? Well, there is one likely answer. Men would be their own gods.

At this point in human history, men seem to be their own divinities. Men make. Men break. Men create. Men destroy. Men do; men don't. Men worship men. Men loathe men. Men are [seemingly] in charge of themselves.

This brings us to an array of existential [if not, dogmatic] questions, to which I am not sure that anyone has answers. Why is God still a thing in a man's world? Why men pray? Why do men have faith? Why men hope? Why men dream? Why men are uncertain of their destiny? Why a man's world is laden with injustice?

If men are [in effect] in charge of themselves, then men should have a place of choice in a man's world. If men are free, then why were they deprived of their freedom? Why would men need to be free? From whom or from which entity, be it a divine being (a god) or else, men gained their freedom? Unfortunately, existentialism provides no epistemological avenues, which would allow us to answer these questions in the most compelling manner.

Let us imagine a world where men are not in charge. Let us explore a world where men are not free. Let us consider a world where men rely on God as much as God relies on men. Let us dissect a milieu where men and God are the same.

PART I

The Shortcomings of Existentialism

1

God is an Existentialist

The intellectual foundation of existentialist theories is the notion that men need no divinity to be free. They need no gods to exist freely on planet earth. Freedom, according to an existentialist approach to human existence, is innate in men. What if it were the contrary?

The understanding is that God, whoever he, she, or it might be, has no significance in a man's world. In refuting God, existentialism, though unintentionally, also recognizes God's existence. The foundation of existentialism is God.

Even though an existentialist perspective to human ontology hints that there is no god, the crux of this theoretical approach relies on God's existence. If there were no God, there would be no need for existentialism. Existentialist ideas are supposed to steer the man away from ill-conceived dogmatic notions.

Another utility for existentialism, I suppose, is to allow men to become their own divinities. Most existentialists would point out a clear divide between men and God. I, on the other hand, would propose the opposite probability.

Dogmatic notions and existentialism go hand-in-hand. One view reinforces the other. When it comes to ideas debating human existence, God is an existentialist. But existentialists do not see God as a reference point to build their own epistemology. Most existentialist theorists see their approach to human ontology as a novel way of looking at the man. Here, I offer a different side of that approach.

For a good portion of the twentieth century, existentialist ideals foreshadowed even the most popular intellectual agreements about the role of God in a man's life. One man [a potent voice in modern philosophy] comes to mind. I am referring to Jean-Paul Sartre.

It is undeniable that Sartre is synonymous with modern literary excellence. Sartrean philosophy is a trademark in contemporary thoughts about human ontology. Sartre was a prominent existentialist.

As a prolific thinker in the field, Jean-Paul Sartre is credited to have created, on his own right, of course, a novel epistemological paradigm about the notion of human existence. The Sartrean approach is the best way, to date, to grasp the nature of humanness. Sartrean philosophy has redefined human ontology. The Sartrean perspective has also undermined human existence, for it provides the intellectual rationale for the rise of anti-humanism.

In the present context, I will not debate the merit of existentialist theories. I will not even refute God to the extent that you might anticipate. I will echo this much though; if you looked closely, you might realize that dogmatic ideals are at the heart of existentialist theories. The same, existentialism is to intellectuals without faith what god is to men of faith. The line between faith-based intellectuals and unabashed men of faith is blurry.

THE FALLACY OF FREEDOM

Existentialism underlies contemporary notions about human freedom. Existential theorists propose the idea that men are free. Otherwise, men have choices. This is a way of saying that men always have spontaneity.

Men could do [or they could omit from doing] whatever they please. But what would that reality implicate? What would it mean to humankind if that were true? Well, it would be the death of God; at least, if God were ever alive.

If men were free to be any manner [or anyhow] they might please, would it not suppose that men would either be God themselves or they would have access to the divine? Freedom [or the notion of individual autonomy] implies that men are omnipotent in the world. Otherwise, they are omnipresent both in the natural and within the artificial. But that characteristic, according to men themselves, is reserved to God.

Before we examine the issues further, let me say that the present analysis is not about God. This discussion is not about earthly deities. Nonetheless, I could not study the being [or the man, for that matter] without considering the foundation of his beingness. That foundation, for all tense and purposes, is God.

I could not ignore the spiritual underpinnings of a man's strength to withstand the blows life throws at him. We should not undermine the roots of a person's thirst for survival. We must recognize that God is an important pillar in a man's plight to make headway beyond a happy accident.

Could we say that God is the source of life in the most fundamental sense? Could we say that God is the Alpha? Could we say that God is the Omega? Where would that reality leave men then? Existentialist theories are mute on these questions.

THE ALMIGHTY MEN

Men of faith are certain that God is supreme. They are convinced that God is ever-present in their world. For them, God [or any being of a divine-like nature] is the provider of life. God [or his kin] gives. God takes back what he gave out.

Let me reiterate that the present diatribe was not designed to refute God. It was not concocted to deny God's existence. This is not a way to undermine God's [supposed] might in the world. But it is important to point out that the reality, which men face on planet earth, at least, most often than you might think, has little or nothing to do with God's will or the lack of that.

In a man's world, some men are almighty. God has no relevance. The divine [or God], if he existed at all, would be an observer. God's will [or God's desire] would matter less; God's words would be of no importance. Let me echo this understanding further to clarify it all.

God is an abstract concept, which has no tangible weight in the reality men face. Every man should aspire to know God. But no man should rely on God too much as a strategy to carve himself a place of choice to survive in a man's world. God, I would proclaim, is a convenient [true] lie, which makes the reality of men livable and, at times, acceptable to the extent that such a reality might be squalid, depressing, or even unbearable.

In the world that most men experience in their quotidian, some men have the status of God. They believe themselves to be divine. Their actions [should I say their inaction] could be as consequential [or the lack of that] as the role that God might play [or might not play] in a man's world.

These individuals often play a crucial role in the destiny of their kind. These men have, most often than you might fathom, more power over their fellow men than any god [imaginary or else] ever could. The divine [or God], in almost every circumstance, is powerless before the depravity of his supposed creations. Here, of course, I am referring to men.

Is it not proof enough that men are [undeniably] Almighty? Is it not obvious enough that men are Lords? Is it not evident enough that men are [definitely] their own gods? You could deny that reality.

BAD FAITH INDIVIDUALS

The world is filled with bad faith individuals. They are determined to tell you a truth that they [themselves] do not know. They are determined to make you believe in the world, which they [themselves] do not believe.

The reality men face in a man's world could be undeniable. Yet some people might claim that God is unparalleled in the world. They might claim that God is the only authority over men. God is an authentic power. From God's heavenly domains, he governs the world.

Some individuals might recite biblical verses to support their arguments. But they might have to convince themselves that God rules a man's world before they could convince others that it is that way. These people do not have the wit to be persuasive. They do not have the pertinent references to convince a true believer to believe in their gospel. A person needs not be persuaded to compel the self to see the world for what it is.

Every truth is self-evident. No truth could be denied as such. Anytime a truth must be taught to others it is because that supposed truth, in and of itself, lacks authenticity or (simply put) is untrue at its core.

In a man's world, the facts are irrefutable when it comes to divinities. There, God is an ideal. God is the figment of our imagination. That imagination is also the result of our desolation in a harsh social milieu. Our tendency to find God is sometimes an indication that we have lost ourselves. It may be a sign that we have lost our sense of self in a world, which we have no means to change. Our craving for God [or our inclination to embrace any divine power] helps us find ourselves amid the chaos, which typifies a man's world.

Let me put it bluntly, God has no tangible power in the real world. Granted, this view is probably in the minority. But the reality, which men face in their daily struggles to stay relevant in a man's world, can be irrefutable. It can be even challenging for a person to stay alive in a man's world. Praying alone could not emancipate men from their own bondage. Men could never be free so long as they must construe their freedom in their own make-believe world.

In a man's world, God is nowhere to be found. There, men are almighty. Some men do whatever they please and to whomever they please. Some men may omit from doing whatever they please and to whomever they please, many a time, with little to no personal consequences. Most men enjoy privileges that are out of this world. But such a lavish existence is supposed to take place in famous testaments only. In a man's world, most men live a life, which the scriptures credited only to God [himself], to god-like beings, to kings, or to a few, but also handpicked, men of faith, whom God purposefully blessed.

In a man's world, the man is against himself. He is also against other beings, which the person may construe as threats to his beingness. The man may see others [or even the self itself] as an impediment to his own existence. But the man who wants to survive beyond chance must find a way to mitigate the reality of the environment where he evolves. Short of complying with this prospect, the man could face premature death.

LIVING IN THE PRESENT

Most existentialists would argue that life is in the present. I do not refute that idea per se. I would echo that view even further. I would say that the man must be attuned to the reality of his milieu. He must make the best out of the living experience. The man must grasp the reality, which he might be witnessing at any point.

While I would not repudiate the notion that men must look after themselves, I could not support the view that men are free to be however they may please. I must recognize that such an understanding is the foundation of existentialist philosophy. At the same time, an existentialist approach to human ontology suggests that men dwell in bad faith when they refuse to accept their reality.

The previous understandings imply than men hold an unparalleled power over their own selves. But if that were to be the case, then it could be said that men are mini gods. Therein lies the incongruency of existentialism.

If men have power over themselves, then why would men need to be free? What could they do with that freedom? How long could a man remain free in a world dominated by other men who desire the same freedom? Whenever one man is free in a man's world, others are unequivocally in a captive state. This is the nature of human relationship.

If two men hold the power to do the same thing, what is the point of that power? If two men are free or if two men could be free, then what is the point of freedom? Freedom is only relevant when others are deprived of it. For one man to be free, others would have to dwell in captivity. Otherwise, freedom would not be an achievement. Rather, it would be a natural state of being. Being free could not be a choice. Being free would be a natural state of being a man.

The real world is not like that. Most men are not free. They could never be that way. If men are free or if they could be that way, then there would be no need for existentialism. There would be no need for God.

The only reason God exists is because men need a divine source of power. Men need to understand their origins. The only reason existentialism is consequential is because God is unattainable in the tangible sense. Hence, existentialism and God must exist in a duality, which is inextricable.

Existentialist theorists are quick to separate men from God. They are also quick to put men on a pedestal like the one god is supposedly standing on. Nonetheless, I would say this much. Existentialists could not have it both ways. It is either the case that men are free to be [however they may please] or they are not that way at all.

Having the potential for freedom means nothing tangible in the real world. Persevering to achieve freedom is not enough to have it in the end. Moreover, freedom, or any sense thereof, is always ephemeral. Thus, men could never be free to the extent that they are men. Men could never be free to the degree that they might want to be that way.

In a man's world, enjoying freedom [or envisaging a similar state of being] is nearly impossible. A state of being, which might resemble an instance of being free is a fantasy. Freedom is superfluous. There is no such thing in the world, let along in the world that men uncover in their mundane.

It could be impossible to distinguish between the reality, which life breeds, and the interpretations of events, which resulted from the actualities that men face in their commonplace. It could be unfeasible to draw between notions debating bad faith and ideas discussing viewpoints about dogmas. No matter what, men must grasp the roots of their calamities in a man's world. They must do so as realistically as possible.

The failure of the man to distinguish between the reality, which society breeds, and the misfortunes, which nature brings about, could have dire outcomes. Ignoring such realities could be deadly. Under any circumstances, the man must be attuned to his nature. The man must become aware of the social conditions, which he might be facing.

Every person must recognize his place in both the natural space and the social place. The man must grasp the essence of the two environments. He must conduct the self fittingly in both his world and the reality, which others experience. He must do so wherever he finds the self.

The man must sense his place in the universe. He should never forego his existence on the count of God or any being, who is believed to be immortal. This is the essence of being in the world. This is also what binds God and existentialism together. The man must understand that reality. Only, he must do so on his own behalf and for his own sake.

2

Appealing to Dogma

Could you say that God is the answer to everything or every situation, which men face in their lives? Many people believe that God is the instigator of everything good in their world. God is there to repulse spiteful beings. To what extent this is the case. I am not sure how to answer.

The pervading viewpoint is that men are caught between two worlds. These spaces, though they are not at all real [or they are not necessarily tangible], include the visible and the invisible. Men have access to these milieux via an introspective portal. Only a man can catch a glimpse of his worlds.

The subjective nature of these places makes them speculative. There is no definite way to tell when a man is in one place or when he is in the other. The links between the two places could be understood as the person's capacity to orate. This is known as *the secret of the oration*.

The invisible world is the foundation of the milieu where the man finds the self. Anything indiscernible to the naked eyes must be plain to see in the invisible world. It is a place of wonder. This is where men are whole.

The invisible world is a place of sanctity. There, God is readily available to those who seek the divine. There, angels guide men through their crucibles. There as well, saints act as overseers of mankind. There, every wish comes true. But it would be that way so long as such a want is conveyed in the proper manner. That manner is a prayer.

In the invisible world, there is no exclusion. There is no discrimination; there is no racism. There, every man is equal. There, men are free. There, men are trouble-free. It is a place of ascension.

Many people pray regularly. They usually rely on God, the one who arts in heavens [or should I say, the one who arts in the invisible world], to guide them through their ordeals on earth [the visible world]. But to what degree God is relevant in helping men mitigate manufactured problems in their lives. What do I mean by made out problems?

Suppose that you evolve in a natural milieu, how easy life would be for you? By using the term "natural" milieu—I mean, suppose that a person evolves in a place where everything is at their natural state. For example, the trees had not been planted by a particular entity—in this case—a person. The flowers grew out of the landscape on their own. The rivers had not been channeled by an exogenous authority or an extraneous mechanism. The stream of freshwater flows as nature intended.

Everything in the natural is there for the taking. Every living being lives off the land. There is a natural progression of life in that milieu. There, survival is not a given; rather, it is available to those who can afford it. In such an environment, would there be a place for God? I will let you ponder on potential answers.

LIFE IN NATURE VERSUS LIFE IN SOCIETY

Every living being was designed to live in the natural. There, life is not superfluous. The living experience is as normal as it could be. Life in nature is not an extraordinary experience.

In the natural, a person would live off the land. He would have an equal chance of survival. The person would thrive like any other living entity would be able to do it.

In the natural state, there would be food. There would be shelter. There would be freedom or there would be some realities akin to that. There would be a milieu, which would be conducive for human beings to evolve. Outside of natural impediments, which characterize the milieu itself, life in that space would be a delight.

In the natural milieu, life would not be based on good luck. The living experience [itself] would not be the result of fortuitous moments. Life would be available to anyone who seeks it. Let us reverse this scenario for a moment.

Suppose we say that you live in a social milieu. How different would life be in that space? A few answers come to mind. But it is undeniable that you would find yourself in a lasting state of despair.

In an artificial milieu, you would struggle to carry out nothing tangible. You and the mundane would become one. Your narcissism would surpass any sense of self you might have. You would be vile; you would be insufferable; you would be nothing but the nothingness itself. You would be vain.

When you find yourself in a social environment, life would have no meaning but what you [yourself] attached to it. You would be petulant. You would be loathsome.

As you uncover yourself in the milieu, you would be arrogant; you would become irrelevant. You would be detached from your own realities. You would ignore your nature, even in the face of it. You would be mentally challenged, for you would seek to deprive yourself of your mental abilities. You would become intellectually inconsequential, for you would rely on others to think for you.

As you become dependent of the milieu, you would lose any sense of self you might have gained in it, from it, or outside of it. You would become violent in your thoughts. You would become lethal in your actions. You would become petty. You would effort to undo anything you could not make out yourself doing.

You would become a destroyer. You would treat others as vermin. You would see them as pests, which must be wiped out at all costs and in all places. You would promote the hatred of your kind. You would become a modern man.

You would pretend to be superior. You would claim ownership over those who could not claim your possession. You would seek to destroy those you may sense as a threat for your dominion of their soul. You would become a capitalist.

You would have no sense of virtue, although you would claim to hold the standard of purity in the world. Your depravity would become the trademark of your conceit for yourself; it would be the same for others. You would live to amass pride.

You would exist for the vanity of the living itself. Your life would mean everything before your eyes. You would dig away [as much as you can] to preserve your existence. You would go to the limit to protect it. You would go from end to end to uphold your beingness. But you would undermine the lives that others experience. You would become an anti-human.

You would see no relevance in the trails a person might be facing so long as such vicissitudes could not help you ameliorate your own life. The life that others experience would be of no significance to your beingness. You would see others as worthless living matters, who should not have been allowed to exist. These individuals would mean nothing to your own survival. You would effort relentlessly to extirpate them from the face of the earth. You would despise them with all your strength. You would smear them to the extent that you could. You would do so even to the extent that you could not undermine them.

You would live an uninteresting life. You would try to build your wealth for the price of your own health or even for that of others. You would have no morals. You would know no deontology. You would have no ethos.

You would embrace the oblivion. You would epitomize the void of your own existence. You would labor solely to satisfy your ego. You would surrender yourself to a state of a lasting decadence. You would become a merciless hero.

You would have no pity for those you banished along your journey to your state of debauchery. You would be lost both in the flesh and in the mind. You would have nothing to offer, but the shameless demand to take anything that belongs to others, to which you would consider yourself the sole heir. You would have nothing to give out, but empty words and platitudes about your greatness. You would become a sous-homme, although you would claim to be great. You would promise to help others reclaim their supposed lost greatness.

STRIVING IN A SUPERFLUOUS WORLD

What might explain the superfluous reality men carve for themselves in a world that was not designed to be special?

The answer could be understood based on our detachment from the natural. At the same time, we would lose our humanity.

Three ideas could explain the reality of men in a world, which is dominated by men, but to the detriment of their own kind. First, there would not be any trees. The environment would be treated as the property of one entity, a person, an agglomeration, or a corporation. Second, everything within the natural would be made-up or it would be artificial. Third, life would not be available. Rather, the living itself would be attainable. But it would be that way only to some. It would be that way only to groups of individuals who are considered worthy enough.

Every man is a member of the human species. As a direct effect of being human, there are no extraordinary beings among us. The tasks that an individual could perform, others could do the same. A few nuances in humanness are worthy of note, though I will not explore them here. But I must point out a few dissimilarities among men.

The notion of humanness itself is not understood universally. Despite our differences [or the potential of that], men are similar at the most intrinsic level. No man is exceptional. Still, we would deny that reality.

Since there are no superhumans among men, the prowess of one man would be tantamount to the strength of the human species. This is the nature of humanhood. We could only be when we can only be. Humanness would be the trademark of our beingness. Some of us could be so long as we can all be.

Finding ways to distinguish oneself from others would be next to impossible. Yet, we would slog relentlessly to do the same. We would try to deny our naturalness. We would undermine our nature. Being in a man's world would be a daunting [if not an impossible] reality to bear.

In the scenario illustrated earlier, a person [or a being] would have to prove himself [or itself] worthy of life. But doing so would be a precondition for the person to be. It would be that way as a condition for others to recognize his beingness. Striving to survive would be a futile endeavor.

The man would have no choice, but to rely on serendipity to exist in a man's world. He would be denied the chance to be every step of his existence. The being must struggle to retain his integrity. It would be supreme for the man to make it beyond a fluke in the milieu where he [or it] finds the self. The individual would suffer simply for being the self. He would endure for daring to be.

The competition would be fierce. Deciphering winners would not be based on a fair metric. It would be hard; else, it would be impossible to distinguish oneself from the rest.

THE TRAGEDY OF BEINGNESS

Humanness is a tragedy. Society [or the visible world] was not designed so everyone could have an equal footing in it. This milieu is based on the misguided notion that everyone is different in their humanness. This reality also makes it possible for some to deny others their humanity.

Society is unjust at its core. This milieu was not designed for everyone to evolve in the same manner. In a social space, men could not be at the same pace or they could not evolve by relying on the same means of survival. The living experience is tailored so some men live a decent life while others rot in a lingering state of abjectness. Society is anti-human. But the reality a man faces in that milieu is by designed.

A social milieu is stratified. Except that it is not based on a natural order of things. Rather, the lamination of the social milieu is *de jour*. It is that way so the barbarity, which characterizes the reality that people face could be seen by those who endure such inhumanity as a normal happening.

The social milieu is gentrified by design. It is that way so actions, which devalue humanhood in their core beingness, can be justified. Society is ranked by design. It is that way, so men feel no need to address the indecency, which pervades within the social milieu itself. Society is unfair by design. It is that way so those who are condemned to live an unjust life could never hold those who receive the better end of the social milieu accountable. Society is unequaled by design. It is that way so those who caused that inequity do not feel overwhelmed [or even overburdened] by those who might make out their social status as the sole cause of the unfair nature of their reality.

In such an environment, men are encouraged to be religious. God becomes a convenient culprit, which many evoke shamelessly to justify the social inequities, which their actions or their omissions bred. In such a place, God becomes the cause of both good and bad. So much as God is righteous, God might be made out as the source of evil.

Society is sorted by design. It is based on standards of human worthiness, which undervalue humanity at its core. It is that way so the devaluation of a man by another has no basis for contestation. Simply put, society is [no ifs and buts] a harmful milieu to every man. The individual did not [or could not] create this reality on his own and for his own.

The social hub is class-conscious. It is codified. It is random; it is unpredictable. It demands an existence of chance. It forces the being to overlook his nature.

Society is an unpredictable milieu. There, human beings have no intrinsic relevance, which they themselves must recognize. Men are [only] what they consider themselves to be. Usually, this is the case at a specific time and, sadly, under specific instances or circumstances. Men are likely to define human worthiness. But manhood itself would be short-lived so it suits a particular tale. Humanity would be nothing but an ideal.

As men would aspire to discover the nature or even the relevance of their humanness, they would also effort to undermine it any chance they get. War would become an element for peace. Greed would become the trademark of human survival. Poverty would be necessary to uphold the status quo. Life would be mundane. But humanhood would be of no importance for the continuity of humanity. As I have just described, these are the characteristics of the social space, which was supposedly designed by men to preserve humankind. This idea is absurd.

Let me say that society is not [by obligation] a bad place for human beings. As an ideal, a social milieu was supposed to be a place where men could mitigate their unwanted nature. It was supposed to be a place where men could suppress their nature to the extent where such a suppression would strengthen the human species. But the social experience has become the source of sorrow in men. Many are unable to cope in that milieu.

The idealism that embodies the creation of a social space is not [in and of itself] flawed at its core. As insinuated earlier, facets of a social environment can be good for humanity. Some people often benefit from being in such a milieu. But it is seldom the case for a majority. I use a proverbial saying to depict those who profit from the social milieu. I refer to them as those who were born with a *golden spoon* in their mouth.

Others must struggle to carry themselves in their milieu. That struggle could be a good thing for the being. He could find a reason to be. The man could give the self *"essence"* in his continuous struggle to tangle.

Because of the reality of a social setting, life may become an endless pursuit. It may never be concretized. Some people would never amount to anything in their milieu. It would be that way so long as they do not fit a particular criterion. Life could become a game of chance.

Those who are born a certain way [or those who grew up in a certain place] would be guaranteed a good living. Others would be denied the same. Those who are made out to lack certain skills would be rebuked. Those who are considered lacking certain qualities would be condemned to plow in vain to endure in the face of the impossible. Their survival would always be unattainable. It would be dreadful. It would be unbearable.

As a mechanism to escape that reality, many would rely on God. This reliance would be symbolized by an insatiable sense of hope. The good life, which God is supposedly epitomized, would only be attainable toward the end of the man's life cycle or long after his death. The person would live to hope; else, he would hope to live.

PART II

The Importance of Hope

3

Living with a False Sense of Hope

In the previously mentioned environment (for example, in a social milieu), hope is the engine of life. It is the essence of the living experience itself. Survival is a secondary asset in men. The primary is resilience. Hope feeds that resilience.

People do not jump through hoops to carry oneself in the milieu where they evolve. Instead, they hope to have the opportunity to struggle to survive. They hope to have the fortuity to live on. Hope is the essence of a man's endurance.

Most people are resilient. They would not falter in the face of calamities. They would not relent in their want to preserve their existence. The problem is that this feature in men could be the source of their downfall.

Human beings are so determined to stay alive that they may lose their essentiality in doing so. They may die during their effort to preserve their beingness. They are susceptible to suggestions, which might be harmful to their own beingness. Some could convince others that their life is worthless. Some might convince others to give up on the self.

In a man's world, resilience could be a curse. Being hardy could be a *barrier* to preserving one's existence in the long run. Those who are aware of that weakness might use it to induce others to self-destruct. Striving to hold out in this world could lead to one's premature death. This is the essence of the calamities, which men face in their journey toward God.

Through that constant struggle to remain whole, the man must make it on his own; else, he must make it for his own; he must make it by himself.

From a man's vantage point, he hopes to have the opportunity to live. All he wants is a decent life. He would endeavor relentlessly to become whole. He would do anything to retain his integrity. Similar individuals would likely cling to life even in the impossibility to do so. They would strive. They would try to maintain their existence beyond happenstance.

These individuals would likely thrive in the face of incommensurable hardships. They would likely find the means to carry themselves in the world. It would be that way regardless of the perfidious nature of the milieu the individual finds the self. The man would become a survivor.

Hope [on its own] is never enough for a man to thrive in a man's world. Similarly, hope is not for everyone. There lies the tragedy of men in a man's world.

HOPELESSNESS AND GOD

In a man's world, there is a relationship between God and resilience. The searches for hope would invariably lead to a need for God. But hope would always be elusive. It would be a barren toil. It would be like trying to distinguish the self from the self. It would be like trying to uproot the self from the natural while claiming ownership of the natural itself.

Without hope, the man often reverted to finding God. Without God, the man reverts to hope. Amid his incertitude, the man wavers between hope and God.

While the man often relies on hope to make it through his journey, he is never certain of his certainty or the lack of that. This reality might explain why God is important in helping the man be in the world. God provides the man a sense of reprieve. The man knows that the matters are not in his hands (in a manner of speaking), at least, should he fail to concretize his dreams. The man surrenders the self to destiny, which is, at the same time, the result of God's will.

I will not discuss the absurdism of this concept in this work. There is no need to delve in the science of faith. But it is worth noting that the man is not even certain that God could give him what he wants, when he wants it, and how he wants it. In it lies the tragedy of hope.

While the man might have hopes, he might also feel a sense of hopelessness in his life. While the man might rely on God, he might not be sure that God could deliver him from his state of everlasting sorrow. He is not sure that God could rescue him from his state of perpetual bondage. But the man does not want to be godless, for being that way would make him anything but a man.

In the face of his calamities, the man often meanders back and forth between hope and faith. The more he hopes, the more he doubts the self. The man often wavers between his fear of God and his fear of meeting his destiny alone.

God is the source of strength in men. So long as the man believes in something, he is going to make an all-out effort to hang on to it. Without hope, God becomes a certainty in man. Without God, hope becomes a source of a man's sense of self.

Hope affords men self-identity. But the line between God and destiny is always blurry. The man often finds the self alone in a man's world. His hope to be a certain way often becomes irrelevant in the face of his brutal reality, which is bred relentlessly (that is, day in and day out) by other men. When hope fades away, so does a man's desire to withstand. Resilience symbolizes a man's inner strength.

In the absence of resilience, self-deprivation or self-deprecation may become a tempting alternative for a battered man. The individual may end up harming himself as he tries to find a means to quench his thirst for reprieve. Under the weight of his horrendous calamities, the man may deprive himself of his [own] self, while thinking this might be the best way to preserve his perceived sanctity in a man's world. The man may end up taking his [own] life in his quest to save himself from the horror, which life breeds in a man's world. In general, God has no say in the terror, which men breed to one another. A man must face the world on his own and for his own. Only a man could save another in a man's world.

ASSESSING GOD'S POWER

Amid a man's ups and downs in this world, he often reverts to finding God as a source of hope. When hope turns into a reality, the man often abandons God. When hope dwindles, the man drifts back to God.

What is it that God could do for a man in a man's world? I would say nothing; nothing at all.

While God may become the essence of hope, he could become the engine of the hopelessness, which characterizes the social reality, which, coincidentally, men are likely to face in their everyday life. In a man's world, God can be useless. God could not help the man beyond a man's wish to help the self.

God has no power in the natural milieu either. I would go as far to say that there is no need for God in the natural. Why would God be an important element in nature? Sadly enough, this ambiguity about the role of God in the world, which men created as a cunning scheme to consolidate their influence over their own kind, is not well understood.

There is a reluctance to address, at least, in a meaningful way, the reality of the humankind. Men do not want to admit their cruelty toward their kind. Even those who are the subject of this horrendous assault are afraid to point out the offenders. This is the nature of the hopelessness, which makes up the reality that men face in their commonplace. This is, to echo, the essence of being in a man's world. This is the reason God often becomes a way out of this squalid social reality. God often becomes a convenient excuse, which men give to themselves, to accept a sordid reality, which the human species was not designed to endure at any stage throughout their existence.

The belief is that God is the key to life in a social milieu. They say that God gives to the man unconditionally. Men also recognize that God could take back whatever he gave them.

As a source of strength, God, many are certain, carries the hands that bless thee. God, some are convinced, is a source of hope. But God, some would also say, is a source of hopelessness in men. God is a disappointment. Nonetheless, for a true believer, there is no substitute for God.

People pray to get (acquerir) what they hope. It is a way to find (trouver) what they want. It is a way for them to have (avoir) what they crave. It is a way for them to keep (maintenir) what they already have.

People do not pray for things that they already have. They do not pray for things that they should have. They do not ask for things that they could have. Rather, people pray for things that they want.

Some may pray for safety. They may pray for security. They may pray for a better life. As people pray for things, which could be considered vanities, they may overlook the real world itself. Their survival [or their incapacity to do the same] often intertwines with their faith in God.

The more a person believes in God, the more likely that the individual would endure. As the person sees God as his only source of strength [or even his only savior], he is likely to accept his reality. As the individual surrenders to God, he is likely to relinquish the self to the whims of the milieu where he evolves. In any case, the man would have a false sense of control over the self.

POSTULATING THE NEED FOR GOD

Who is God? Where did this notion emanate? There is no definite answer. Many people would agree that God is the most powerful being in the universe.

What is the relationship between God and society? Finding answers could be next to impossible.[1] Even so, one could make the case that society created God, if not, this milieu provides the rationale for God's existence.

In a social milieu, God is indispensable. There, God provides certainty in an uncertain world. God provides peace and tranquility, even in the most tenebrous times.

For most people, God is their only source of hope. Praying may become an essential facet of self-preservation. It might be a way to uphold what one already has. It could be a way to seek what one wants.

Some people pray for more. Others pray for less, depending on what more is or what less is for them [or what either one of them could be]. The same person could pray for more wealth, while he prays for fewer problems. The individual might pray for fewer complications in life for the self, while hoping for the opposite for someone else.

Misunderstandings about God may lead to a sense of hopelessness. It could induce the person to lose his faith in God. The person may feel abandoned. He may renounce God altogether. He may lose his spiritual foundation.

---

[1] Please refer to the book titled *Crime and Nature* to learn more about this concept.

This reality could lead the individual to lose his footing in the world. It could also lead the person to engage in conducts, which might lead to his premature death. The person could suffer from the reality he normally faces. But he would lack the spiritual pillar to hang on.

The man may falter in the face of his misfortunes. He may not be able to deal with unforeseeable life's hurdles, including financial difficulties, diseases, loss of a loved one, and other run-of-the-mill problems, which he might have faced differently had he kept his faith in God. The individual may lose his health; he may lose his wealth.

In a social milieu, to echo a previous viewpoint, God is often made out to be both a creator and an exterminator. People appeal to God for both the good and the bad. The belief is that God is an omnipotent force. God sees everything; he knows everything.

In a man's world, God is often made out as a caring being. For most men of faith, God is filled with compassion; God understands the plight of men. God feels the suffering of the human species. God decides the nature of the being. God fixes the extent of the man within the social milieu. God, some are certain beyond a shred of a doubt, epitomizes the man in the most intrinsic sense. But is that really the case? Let us explore God's role in a man's life from a practical lens.

4

Blaming God

If God is omnipresent in a man's world, what would be the source of human suffering? Does God have a responsibility in the distress that men experience? Is God to blame when men deny their kind the right to be? What role God should play in making life livable in a world seemingly designed to take life away from the bearer of it? We could sketch out the nature of human suffering in several categories. Here, let us focus on two facets.

The first one could be described as natural suffering. The second could be understood as social suffering. The former is not suffering, at least not by itself. Rather, it is the circumstances of life itself.

The latter is more complex to make out. It is often induced by social conditions, which the man could not escape. It is also a calamity for the being. The man is not equipped with the *savoir-faire*, which would enable him to mitigate the sordid situations, which he faces in his quotidian.

Regardless of the reality that the man faces, he always reverts to God. Whether or not he is a believer, the man always doubts the self. Doubt is also the fastest path to God or to a divinity.

Doubt is certainty, for it puts the doubter on notice. The doubter is certain of nothing but his [own] confusion. The more the man doubts, the more he becomes certain of his lack of certainty. The man becomes certain of a gap between what is and what could be. That gap could only be filled by destiny.

When good things happened to the man, he credits his good fortunes to God. When bad things happened to the man, he blames God [or God's nemesis].[2] In blaming God, the man also blames the self for not surrendering himself to God's will. Either way, the man doubts.

Amid his calamities, the man is not sure whether God is punishing him or whether God is building him. But the man is always certain of his misgiving about the role God supposedly played in his crucibles in life.

The man understands that he lacks certainty. He is certain of nothing but his own doubt. That certain confusion (or doubt) is the foundation of the man, for it provides him a sense of self. The man always reverts to his certainty of his [own] misgiving about his world.

The more the man finds out about the self, the more he doubts the self. The more he doubts the self, the closer he gets to God. The closer he gets to God, the closer he gets to the self, for he realizes that all he is [in this world] can be summed up in one word, God. Yet, the man is not certain of his discovery. He feels a constant gape in his life.

The more the man yearns for meaning, the least confident he becomes about his discoveries about the self. The more he learns about the self, the more confused he becomes about the self, for the self keeps eluding him. God

---

[2] In biblical terms, God's nemesis is Satan [or the evil].

becomes a bridge between the self and anything else. God fills the gap between the real and the surreal. God restores the man, for, according to the man himself, God makes him whole. The man only finds solace in God. So, he prays.

While the man blames God for his misfortunes, he praises God for his providence. The man finds confidence in the self only when he surrenders himself to God or to a made out divine power. God often becomes an important force, which carries the man in his infinite search for meaning.

In essence, God provides the man a sense of self. God guides the man through the crucibles of life. God often becomes the man's only *Sheppard* on this desolate stretch of land called earth.

The freedom that Jean-Paul Sartre speaks of comes from God. Men could not be free unless God gave them the ability to be that way. Men could not be their own owners if it were not for God's believed ownership of their soul. Thus, God and existentialism, to reiterate it here, go together.

God is the source of freedom in men. Without God, men could not make out what it means to be free. Without God, men could not consider themselves being free. Without God, men would remain in an everlasting state of captivity, at least in the mind. God makes it possible for men to emancipate themselves from one another. By any seeming, God is also an existentialist, for without God, men could not extirpate themselves from the natural.

Without God, men would not know what it means to seize one another. Without God, men could not envisage any sense of freedom. For men, God is a model for both good and bad. That is why God is important for men in a man's world.

THE REALITY OF LIFE

In the natural, every human being is equipped with the tools to survive. The person has the *know-how* to deal with misfortunes of life. He has what it takes to face the sorrow and the pain, which life brings to his front doors. Here, I am referring to physical distress or emotional hardships.

The man was designed to suffer. But nature equips the person with the means to endure. The man has what it takes to resist. He has what it takes to deal with the hard life. The man has the means to subsist on his own. The problem is that such aptitudes are denied to the man in a social milieu.

The man is condemned to struggle in vain in society. There, he is doomed to fail. The man is destined to suffer in futility in a man's world. This is the irrefutable tragedy of the life, which men experience regularly in their own world.

An important category of suffering worth considering here is mental hardships. This suffering, though intangible, may include psychological anguish, which could be excruciatingly painful. The man was not set up to bear indiscernible realities. This type of suffering often comes from society. The man is caught between two worlds.

The man must learn to cope with the substance of his social milieu. Otherwise, he might lose control of the self in that environment. The man might die prematurely. Then again, the man could not cope with his reality. He often meanders back and forth between the real and the surreal. In the end, the man may lose the self in the search for it.

Human suffering, at least in a social milieu, did not originate from God. It did not come from the natural either. God could have little or no power over human sorrows in a man's world. God did not invent society; at least, the divine did not do so in the most material sense; God did not create the social milieu; at least, not in its current form.

GOD AS A HERO

God could not be the source of your happiness. God could not reward you the beautiful house you have dreamed about. God could not give you the splendid yacht, which you wanted your whole life. God could not make you rich; God could not make you smart; God could not make you prosperous. Still, many people believe that God is going to rescue them from their socially induced woes. Would that be the case? I would say no; not at all, I might add.

Thinking that way is illogical. Yet, this is the foundation of a man's faith in a world, which only needs him to be brave so he could fend off the tumults that he might face in his quotidian. The world requires the man to believe in the self and not in some make-believe superpower entity, for the tangible nature of the world itself is plain.

For most men of faith, God is the creator of the universe. From their vantage point, God controls everything. He has full power over everyone. This view is also irrational. It places God before anything else. It even places God before men. As I have sought to show here, this is not the case at any point in human history.

Claiming that God [and only God] oversees the world is shortsighted. At best, this viewpoint is a romantic understanding of the world that we experience. At worst, this opinion is proof of our obliviousness of a milieu, which was designed to undermine our beingness in it.

Men are the overseers of themselves. Men even claim to oversee the natural. Men see themselves as omnipotent. Men consider themselves the sole owners of the planet. In effect, society is a well-crafted machine, which was designed to undermine men. God [if God there is] has no say about which men are. Despite the natural, men are whoever they might want to be. In it lies the tragedy of human existence.

Men are far from being who they always claim to be in this world. In the most obvious reality, men are insignificant beings. In the natural milieu, men control nothing but themselves. But even that control is short-lived. Men have power over their kind only to a certain extent.

Despite what men think of themselves, they enjoy lasting dominion over nothing in the natural. Men have no tangibility beyond what nature affords them. Thus, men enjoy no power in the milieu where they evolve. Claiming otherwise would reveal our lack of capacity to realize the nature of our [own] nature. It would be a mistaken approach to the reality of men in their world.

THE NATURAL RULES

A bitter reality about the relevance of men in the natural milieu is worth considering as we move along here. Nature always rebukes a man's view of his reality. The place that men claim to hold in the natural is real to the extent that nature would allow it. But the natural milieu always refutes a man's belief about his omnipotence or his omnipresence.

Whatever men think about their kind nature refutes it. To support the view that God rules the world, many have sought to draw a line between nature and God. They have sought to draw a wedge between a social and a natural milieu.

Those who hold strong religious beliefs [or those who believe in God] are certain that the divine is always there for them. The man has no need to worry, they say. God got his back. The man has no need to be concerned about the world itself. God will protect the man in that deceitful milieu.

Many people are convinced that God is watching over them. There is no need for essence, they say. There is no need for freedom, some are certain. Most men of faith are convinced that only God oversees the world. Whatever your anguish might be, bring them to God, they say. God alone, many are certain, has the solution to the world's problems. Is that the case in substance? This is not so, I would say.

I have a different outlook about the role of God in the world that men know in their quotidian. I do not think that God exists to help one group to the detriment [or even to the demise] of another. I could not see the role of God that way. I could not see the world from such a myopic lens. I do not think that God could have an influence on the reality of men in an artificial milieu [society]. In saying that, I reckon that God could be a source of inner strength for most people.

The belief that many people hold in God could help them endure. It could help them face their calamities of the real world. To echo a previous understanding, God is a source of certainty in an uncertain world.

A man's beliefs about God could help him face the world in its most tangible realities. In any case, I doubt that God has any power over men. If God held some power over the humankind, it would not be in the most physical sense.

5

God is in the Sky

Many people are searching for God. The first place they always look for the divine is the sky. It is unlikely that God would be in one location. Finding God in the sky is an antiquated notion about where God is located [or where the divine could be].

Men have always held misguided beliefs about realities, which they could not make out on their own. When people believed that the earth was flat, many were convinced that the earth had always been that way. We know now that the earth has always been spheric. The same could be said about the notion that God is in the sky. God's location is unknown.

The belief that God is in the sky is integral to believing in God. To believe that God is in the sky is to believe in God himself. Even though men have been in space and have seen—firsthand—the vastness of the universe, the common belief about God being in the sky perdures. The notion that this is where God is [or should be] lingers.

I do not want to undermine notions about God's location in any way, shape, or form, for I could not pretend to know where God is. I could not even tell you where nature is. I do not have such insights. I doubt that God is anywhere men could envisage or even imagine in a clear state of mind.

Saying that God is in the sky is the most tangible proof we hold of God's existence. After all, the sky is visible. We could debate the nature of the sky itself. We could point out the intellectual opacity of the notion. Then again, I must also concede that faith is important in a man's life.

Believing that God is in the sky is the foundation of a man's faith in the divine. I could not challenge that idea, for I reckon that most people hold that view dearly. The belief that God is in the sky is held by most religions.

BELIEFS AND GOD

Would it not make sense to deduce that there might not be a sky, at least, in the most tangible sense? Could it be true that the blue space, at times gray, white, or even black, is not where God is? Could we see the sky as a physical representation of an empty space, which forms the universe itself?

Suppose we say that there is a sky. Could we also claim [at least, without a shred of a doubt] that this is where God lives? Could we make such an assertion without relying on faith?

Certain facets of a belief are important for that belief to hold. Believing in God [or believing any divine entity] demands not only faith, but also good faith. The believer must genuinely believe in the belief itself. This is the underpinning of any belief; be it religious or else.

As a believer, you must have faith. You must believe in your belief to believe. You must not only believe in some entity, but you must also believe in your belief to believe in the entity.

To believe, the believer must believe even in the most ridiculous ideas about the supposed entity to which he believes. Doing so shows the man's good faith to have faith. Faith, as I try to explain here, can be damaging for the man.

The more the man believes, the more he learns about the reason that he believes. He also learns about the nature of the source of the belief itself. The more the man learns about the reason for his beliefs and the nature of the entity, to which he believes, the more likely he would lose faith in the reason that he believes or the reason that he must believe.

The belief itself often becomes a source of turmoil in the person. Overtime, the belief that the person holds about the self or others, including the divine, subsides. The person becomes a doubter.

When it comes to survival, the notion of faith can be harmful to a person's well-being. The individual may forfeit the self to a reality, which has no concreteness beyond a subjective sense of what truth is or what such a reality could be. It is not surprising that most believers live in a state of constant depravity in a man's world. They think that God will rescue them from their misery. This is absurd.

RELIGION AND GOD

Existentialism says that there is no god. Is it a verity that there is no God? I do not know what to tell you. Here is what I know. Existentialists do not know either. In fact, no one knows whether there is a god [or not]; at least, no one knows that factuality; no one knows of the possibility of that; at least not for sure.

Religion, in contrast, says the opposite. From a religious vantage point, there is a god. In fact, you must surrender to that God, they say.

The divine is the answer to all your troubles. All you need to do is to find God; you must bring him your woes. God will make them disappear. Is that true? To be honest, I do not know for sure.

Then again, here is what I know. I have problems. I have always had them. My problems seem endless. No matter what I do, my problems are always there.

I have prayed to God. I have asked for my problems to go away. I am sure you have done the same. Have your problems been solved. My problems have not been solved. On the contrary, my hurdles seem to be multiplying.

Does that mean that God has ignored my prayers? Does that mean that I do not know how to pray? Does that mean that I am not a believer? I will leave these questions open, for I am certain that you have them too.

Men of faith would have you believe that you must be patient. God is slow to act. God is kind and generous. Give God time, they say. This is absurd.

Existentialists, on the other hand, would tell you that there is no god. You must take matters into your own hands. You must take charge of your own destiny. Is there a shred of truth to these views? I will let you be the judge of that.

I would say that God is an ideal in a man's world. Despite God's presumed relevance in helping men navigate their reality, the divine has no clout in a man's world. Even if there were a God, I doubt that religion would be a path to that divine entity. I am perplexed that men of faith could lead you to any god, for being men could be a barrier to any divinity. Men are impure in their core beingness. Men know no purity.

6

The Corruption of Faith

Every religion is corrupt at its core. Every faith-based approach to human reality must be coercive, for it requires men to overlook his [own] nature. Religion is a path away from God, for it is a path that takes men away from themselves.

Religion demands that the man stops to be. This is a condition for the men to find God. Yet, the same religion proclaims that men are the creation of God. But they could not have it both ways.

Religion, regardless of its origins or its dogmatic setup, is a tyrannical tool, which came about to undermine men in their nature. Religion, in all its glory, corrupts men in their made-out sense of purity. Religion, despite its proclaimed sanctity, destroys men simply for being men.

From a religious lens, to find God is to lose oneself to the unknown. Yet, religion offers no tangible solutions, which could help men deal with some of the most pressing problems they face in their quotidian. Religion, regardless of its appearance [or regardless of its purpose, be it real or made out], is a farce. It emblematizes our incapacity to make out the nature of our own nature. Invoking the name of God is a convenient contrivance to induce men to surrender the self to other men.

Religion is an unnecessary load, which men must carry during their crucible in this world. It is useless; at least, to the extent that the man understands his own reality. Religion offers men nothing perceptible, which would enable them to further their own existence.

My point is that even if you are a believer, you should not limit yourself to what others tell you about your own truth. Look around you and see your reality for yourself. You need no priest to help you uncover [or even to discover] yourself. You need no ordained minister to help you find your way in a place, which you know like the palm of your hands. You need no prophet to guide you through your own path. You need no guru to tell you about your own reality. You need no pastor to show you the light, for he could not see it. You need no imam to tell you about your journey toward the nirvana, which he has no clue about where to find it. You need no god to help you live your life; a life, which God himself, supposedly awarded you in the first place.

To survive in this world, you need to be you. To make it whole in a man's world, you need to do so on your own. To survive beyond chance in this treacherous milieu called earth, you need to embrace your reality as is. To be yourself, you need to be you as much as you are.

In the face of your social calamities, you must hold on to your god. The divine may become the source of your strength to withstand the blows of life in a man's world. You must pray. You must hope. You must also continue to doubt.

They say that the almighty god is in the sky. As discussed earlier, this is unlikely the case. Nothing material [or even spiritual] suggest such a likelihood. Then again, the science of faith is not on trial here. Nonetheless, we must reexamine the science of fate. We must reevaluate our understandings of the divine or its origins, for that matter. To do so, we must ask ourselves in all sincerity, where is God then? How do we find God? Could we even find God?

FINDING GOD

I do not know where God is. Even so, I am certain that God, if that entity existed at all, it would not be in one place; at least, this is not as most believers seem convinced that it is. I am perplexed that God [whoever that entity is or could be] is static somewhere in the universe. It is probable that God [if God there is] would not be in the sky. The reality of God would not be in the same way that most people believe it to be.

Even if God were in the sky, would it mean that he would be in one place? The answer is no, for we know the earth is turning around. Every second, there is a different sky. As a result, God's location would not be up there. If there were a sky [in the most tangible sense], it would be everywhere. That sky would be visible to every man.[3] God would know of the pain and misery of every man or that of every living being on the planet.

It does not make sense to invoke the name of God as the only way to carry the self. God would have no concrete

---

[3] There would not be the same sky from either Mars or the Moon.

power over men. The man must accept that reality. He must do so if he wishes to survive beyond the stars.

The man must fathom the nature of the world. He should not rely on faith or on fate to outlast everything else or anyone else. He should develop the faculty [or the capacity] to negotiate real forces in the natural, which might be lethal for him. The man must have an edge in the natural.

The man must be in control of his destiny. He must be free to be within the limits of his nature. I admit it here; this is a grandiose way of looking at the world. The man is weak-minded. He has no control over his realities, be they social or else.

The man is malleable in the social milieu. Before the man could master his mental prowess [that is, even his spiritual strength], he would have to be devoid of it. That is why God is important for the being.

Despite the possibility that there might be a god, who might be omnipresent and omnipotent, the man would still be responsible for the self in a man's world. He must be down to earth. The man must become attuned to his reality. His survival may depend on that realization.

THE REALITY OF THE WORLD

To understand the reality of the world, we must grasp the link between faith and fate. These understandings are the foundation of human existence in a man's world. The underpinning of this worldview is that men exist by faith or they exist by fate.

Men exist by faith when they allow themselves to become the tools of God. In this instance, men are not free to be. Men are the product of an overseer, God. Men are not themselves. They dwell in an eternal state of bad faith.

By contrast, men exist by fate when they create their own destiny. In other words, men make up their own fate. Men are free to be who they want to be. Under this presumption, existence always precedes essence.

While the former understanding is mostly echoed by men of faith (or religious zealots), the latter is the creation of existentialist theorists, such as Jean-Paul Sartre, at least in modern philosophical writings. But both approaches are in error. Both understandings remove men from their own realities. It is as if the real world did not apply to men.

There ought to be a third approach. Here, I propose the understanding that men must survive. Men must realize that they are not alone in this world. They must concretize that survival is promised to no one in the natural. But to avoid a life of chance or serendipity, men must grasp their reality in its most displeasing state. This is the nature of the real world.

Existentialism refutes God unequivocally. Still, those who propose such an understanding of the world itself are uncertain of its veracity. Existentialism solidifies the science of faith. But it does so under the guise of intellectual purity.

Under any circumstances, no existentialist theories could support their notions about God's existence or the lack of that. To be an existentialist is to believe in not believing in God. There is no certainty in existentialism.

The only way that an existentialist could be certain of his [own] existence is for him to doubt that existence. Hence, every existentialist must have faith in their belief to not believe. Then, what sets an existentialist apart from a zealous religious fanatic? What sets an atheist or even an agnostic apart from a religious zealot? On the face of it, nothing, nothing at all.

Existentialist theorists believe that there is no god, period. You [the man] must oversee your [own] destiny. But you must oversee yourself in a world where you have no materiality. You must be even in your incapacity to be.

What the previous understanding presupposes is that men are [or should be] responsible for themselves in a world, which they did not demand to become a part of. Whatever the man does [or does not do] is that he must endure. Whatever a man does not [do] is for him to experience on his own and for his own.

Men of faith offer a different perspective. From their vantage point, there is a god. As such, a man has no power other than what God affords him.

From a religious viewpoint, the understanding is that men are not in charge of themselves. They are not free, though they could be. Men must abdicate the self to God.

According to that worldview, men are God's creations. Their sole purpose on this earth is to worship God. As a result, men have no tangible freedom, which does not come from God himself. Men could not be [or they could not do] according to their own choosing. Men must follow the scriptures. Men must obey the words of God.

On the one hand, I would say that both approaches are misguided. By contrast, I would say that they are relevant as well, depending on the circumstances. Men need both the self and his god to make it in this world. Every man must consider both approaches to further his own existence. Short of that, the man would perish prematurely. The man would never know the good life. The man would live in an eternal state of misery.

Freedom alone could not emancipate men from their mental [if not, their spiritual] bondage. God could not undo what men did to themselves. A person must be practical. This is the crux of the philosophy of survival. This is what it means to be a survivalist in a man's world.

BEING A SURVIVALIST

There are more than a few misconceptions about survivalist philosophy. Survivalism is misunderstood to mean anything but what it is [in substance]. Being a survivalist has little or nothing to do with one's capacity to make it in this world when others could not.

A survivalist is not the person who has stocked the right amount of food. A survivalist is not the person who knows how to thrive in the wild. A survivalist is not the one who has the guns or other machinery, which would make it easier for the person to survive. A survivalist is not the one who knows how to make it whole in horrendous conditions. Instead, a survivalist is the one who understands the importance of survival.

A survivalist needs not to carry loads of food or other items to survive. A survivalist is the person who knows how to make food. He knows where to find food; he knows why he must eat at a particular moment.

A survivalist needs no gun to survive. A survivalist is the person who knows how to avoid being in the place when a gun might be necessary to survive. A survivalist needs no special skills to survive. Rather, a survivalist understands the need to survive in the world beyond chance.

To be a survivalist is to be aware of the self in the world. Sadly, few people have such a capacity. Most people would endanger themselves in trying to preserve it. Being in the world requires the person to be a survivalist.

If you are evolving among lions and tigers, you must catch the drifts of these animals. You must be conscious about these beasts in your milieu. You must grasp your own nature.

It might get to a point where a lion might make you out as food. The lion might see you in a way, which would enable it to further its own existence. You might become a meal for that lion.

As you evolve among lions, you must be aware of that reality. That awareness might help you find out whether you could weather your troubles long enough among these flesh-eating creatures, for you are made of flesh. The failure of you to come to that realization could be fatal.

God may not be able to prevent you from being consumed by a lion, especially if you were to cross the path of a hungry lion when he is hunting for food. It could be the case if you found yourself in a place where a lion is protecting its territory. The question remains, where would God be? How could God help the man improve his life in the natural or in a social milieu?

Despite these paradoxical interrogations, it would be unwise to dismiss the power of God in the life of a believer. For most devotees, God acts in mysterious ways. His actions could be tangible for some people. God's influence in the world, which some men experience, could also be elusive for others.

It is always important for a man to remain down-to-earth. It is always important for a man to be open-minded in a man's world. It is always crucial for the individual to be aware of the self in the world. I learned that from my grandmother Yvette.

My grandmother was a survivor. She sustained herself all the way through the last seconds of her life. She was a survivalist like the world never seen. My grandmother is the foundation of my philosophy in life.

PART III

Growing up among Believers

7

My Grandmother and God

When I was a child, I remember that my grandmother Yvette (Vetto) was firm about the power of God in her life. She was confident of her beingness. Vetto always said that she would know the day of her death. Indeed, she knew of that day.

Vetto was a survivalist, though she did not see herself that way. Vetto relied on her instincts to survive. She used to say that there is no such a thing as chance.

Vetto always said that everything is something. Even nothing is something. She said that nothing happens by coincidence. There is always a reason for everything, even the perceptible instances and the ones that are not perceptible.

In this world, Vetto used to say, every action causes a reaction. Whether that action [or that reaction] is perceived in one way or another is never inconsequential. But it is up to the man to understand the world around him. He must grasp the reason events occurred; he must understand the reason events unfolded the way that they did. He must also grasp the reason events did not take place in an expected manner. The man must get at the bottom of the reason that the world is the way that it is.

Vetto had a hunch for every situation. She sounded prophetic at times. It was as if she could sense the future. Her dreams were vivid. They were psychedelic. They were revelatory of days to come.

My grandmother's forebodings would come true in the most intense manner. Her intuitions were always on point. Her omens often revealed real moments, which often left neighbors bewildered.

Vetto often relied on her bodily exhibitions to express her fears and her concerns. She believed that these expressions suggested upcoming events or events occurring incognito within the natural. As a child, I thought Vetto was superstitious. I often dismissed her concerns or her advice. She often reminded me that I lacked faith in myself.

When a dog barks, Vetto would say that there is a reason for that. When it rains, Vetto would say that there is a reason for that. When it does not rain, Vetto would still say that there is a reason for that.

Vetto used to say that the human brain is not innately aware of anything. The person must train the self to become aware of the self. The person must learn to become attuned to his nature. This is the essence of survival. Every living being must become in touch with the natural. Otherwise, the being would perish without knowing why.

Vetto had a body sign for everything that might transpire during the day. She was confident in her ability to sense danger anywhere. She used to tell me to follow my instincts in every situation. She was not the only person I knew at the time who felt that way.

LIVING AMONG BELIEVERS

When I was growing up in Haiti, most people I knew in my surroundings were survivalists. Yet, many of them believed in God. Others believed in something else. Often, it was a spiritual being or a *Lwa*[4] (in Haitian Creole), whom many believed had godlike powers. I did not grow up among non-believers.

Many people in my life believed in their capacity to see the world from a different perspective. I must admit that I did not understand what that meant. I could not believe that these individuals would enjoy what you might call superhuman abilities. I did not think this was even possible.

I would hear the term "instincts" being echoed around me. I would hear people claim that my instincts told me to do this; my instincts told me not to do that. I did not think that I could be that way. I did not think that I had an instinct. I could not fathom this concept in the practical sense.

As I grew older, I began to experience weird feelings about my surroundings. I would have peculiar bodily signs about events to come in my life. I would feel the same for people around me. I would sense when something good is about to happen. I would feel the same when something bad is about to happen to me or to someone close to me.

---

[4] The term "Lwa" is Haitian creole for spiritual beings. In Haitian voodoo religion, a lwa is a spirit (good or bad) who oversees the people of the land.

I would have feelings of joy, even when I had no immediate reasons to be happy. Even though I would doubt my emotions [or my forebodings] something would happen later that day or the following day, which would corroborate my bodily anticipation. When I experienced feelings of joy, something would happen to me later that day, which would make me feel happy.

I would anticipate painful moments in my life. I would foresee sorrowful days. I would experience feelings of an impending doom, even when I had no reason to worry. I knew that my body was reacting to nature in ways that I could not fathom or even make out with the naked eyes.

I learned to communicate with the natural. I learned to tap into that source of strength whenever I was not sure of myself. I learned to listen to myself. I learned to listen to the natural milieu through my own senses.

As I learned to listen to the natural, I realized that Vetto did not have superhuman powers after all. She knew how to communicate with the natural. But she had no special skills. When I was old enough to understand my social realities, I was doing the same.

Over the years, I learned to develop a more intimate knowledge of my nature. I learned to see the entities around me not with my eyes, but with my senses. Doing so revealed a world to me, which I could not have envisaged by relying solely on the spectacles, which others placed before my eyes.

A Personal Lens

As a grown man, I could say that I am savvy of my reality, be it social or else. Perhaps I am too confident in myself now. Perhaps you would call this sentiment a sign of my immaturity. Okay, I would not refute your assessment of my understanding of my own world.

I, too, am not certain of my reality. More often than I thought, I would admit it without shame in this instance, I doubted myself. More often that I realize, I doubt myself. I am certain of nothing about myself in my world. But I would point out that doubt can also be a source of certainty.

What I have learned about myself is that the more I doubt, the more certain I become of my doubts. I am certain that I know nothing about myself. I am certain that I know nothing about my world. I am also certain that I know nothing about God. That is the beauty of my circumstances.

Every day, I toil exhaustingly to uphold my doubt about myself, for that doubt is the source of my want to preserve my beingness. Since I am certain of nothing, I am always certain of my misgivings. That state of doubt gives me a sense of self, for it reinforces my view of the world or the lack of that. I understand my fragility even in the face of my made-out strength in it. My doubt brings me down to earth.

The more you doubt, the more certain you become of your doubts. As you doubt, you are unlikely to overlook realities, which might be contrary to your expectations. As you doubt, you become whatever it is that you doubt. Doubt gives you insights about the world.

Faith undermines a man's capacity to doubt. As the man tries to evince his doubt, he may become oblivious to the reality, which might be flashing right before his eyes. Faith demands the man to be a believer. But belief turns the man into a blind with no sense of self in a world where being along could be a reason to lose oneself.

BEING A BELIEVER

I was once a believer. I had an optimistic view of the world. As a child, I had a romantic understanding of the people in my milieu. I grew up in a religious family. For a good portion of my life, I had a literal interpretation of the bible. I did not think the world was so bad.

I knew that there were bad people in the world. I knew of the existence of evil or even the devil. But I had a quixotic view of human relations on earth.

When I went to church on Sundays, I saw that people were always embracing each other. Often, as I witnessed this reality, they did so with complete strangers.[5] Somebody would always drop something in a beggar's hands. I knew that there was love among the people of the world.

As I grew older, my faith in God grew stronger. I became convinced that there was a clear divide between good and bad. But that view was mostly fueled by my religious upbringing. It was the result of my understanding of stories, which I had heard from others about the world.

As a child, I rationalized those tales to be the only truth in the world. Granted, I did not understand what they meant in the real world. I must also admit that my views of the world were perverted on purpose.

My whole life, I had been told lies about the world. I had been led to believe that I was a part of the world. I was told that I was responsible for what was happening in the world. They said that I had a say in my world. I had to speak up; I had to be proactive, they said.

After getting the same lecture from different individuals, including my parents, my friends, my neighbors, my

---

[5] I grew up in a religious environment. Many relatives were Catholics. I was raised in the Catholic faith as well.

schoolteachers, and even from the books I read, I started to believe that I was playing a role in my own destiny. I started to believe that I, in some ways, played a role in the reality that others experienced in their quotidian.

The more I understood that I was responsible for what was happening either to me or to those around me, the more I felt the need to protect both myself and others. I thought I had the rights to be. I thought others had the rights to exist. I wanted to help make the world a better place. But I was turning into an egotistical hero.

FALSE HEROES

In my early twenties, I was so naïve that I was looking forward to a good life. I thought that I could amount to anything I wanted in this world. All I had to do was to apply myself. I bought in the idea that the sky is the limit.

At first, I did not see anything wrong in being a part of the world. I thought it was noble to be a part of the story of the human species. I did not see anything wrong in being a protector of human's good nature. I saw nothing wrong in fending the world against evil [real or made out]. As I grew older, my attitudes changed. I became a cynic.

I would admit that my views about the world, though I thought they were my own, were [in fact] the results of others. They emanated from the popular culture, which surrounded me during my upbringing. I could not see the world for what it was [or for what it is].

I thought that the world had characters, such as Batman, Zorro, Superman, Robin Hood, Harry Callahan, Rocky Balboa, and Indiana Jones, just to name a few. I thought that the *"good guys"* were always good. I grew up with a television mindset. I expected that every situation would have a *"happy ending."* I learned that the real world was often the opposite.

When I became an adolescent, I was shocked to find out that the real world is cruel. As I started to make sense of the milieu where I found myself, I learned that the planet itself was distasteful. It had individuals with questionable characters. I learned that these people often ruled their social milieu [or crucial facets of it] with rigor. They often have no mercy for the poor; they have no pity for the weak; they have no regards for the gentiles.

I learned that bad was more prevalent than good; evil was always likely to prevail. I saw that good was always unlikely to make a difference in a man's world. Evil would always win, I thought. I saw this reality as the trademark of the world, which I could not uncover on my own, at least while I was a young man. Little by little, I became a doubter.

In making these assertions, I am not hinting that I am a pessimist. I do not know what it means to be a nihilist, for I have never been that way. I understand what it means to believe. I grew up among believers.

My beliefs have also changed me. They turned me into a realist. Now, I can see the world for what it is. This place is lethal for a man to evolve. I do my best to preserve myself in this deceitful place. I strive to the extent that I could do so. This is the only way, I think, I could see another day. So, I strive in the oblivion to maintain my existence.

8

Becoming a Doubter

I do not [or I could not] view the world from a lens other than my own. But the prism through which I view my world reveals a disheartening world. It is, to say the least, a depressing milieu.

As I uncovered myself in the world, I saw the treacherous nature of this milieu. I saw the dishonesty that characterizes this place. I saw the maliciousness that lingers in the heart of my fellow men. I became afraid of them. I became angry at them. I feel no pity for them. I am prepared to face them.

I realized that the best way to survive in this world is *not to find the self* on the wrong side of certain men. They have the means to hurt others. They have a license to kill. They have the will to be evil; they have the fortitude to hurt you in your core being. They would not care about what they might be doing to you. They would justify their injustice toward your soul by referencing all sorts of lies.

Others would repeat such mendacities until you devalue your [own] self. Such dishonesty would be echoed by people who are supposed to know better. They would repeat such lies until they become engrained in your psyche. You would be reduced to a state of nothingness.

Once you have rationalized your state of insignificance, you would see no worth in your own beingness. You would accept your state of nothingness. You would surrender yourself to the savagery, which you are forced to endure in your quotidian. You would surrender your soul to the hatred, which epitomizes the milieu where you evolve. You would abandon yourself to the impulses of others.

As I became more mature, I realized that there is a fine line [if not a blurry stroke] between good and bad in modern societies. I learned that good or bad is often relegated to the actor, the person being acted on, the beholder, the sufferer, or the *"Profiteur"* or the person profiting from the actions that are being perpetrated onto another.[6] I began to see the world for what it is.

As I started to doubt men's capacity to sketch between good and bad, I became certain of their incapacity to resist bad. I saw that men could not reach the state of perfection, which they expect from themselves. I saw that men could never be as righteous as they claim to be.

The more I realized the lack of virtue in men, the more I became wary of the sanctity of my own beingness in a corrupt milieu. I became certain of the incapacity of men to achieve the purity, which some desperately seek in themselves and in others. The more I looked for virtue in men, the more I realized their lack of it.

As I experienced the world for what it is, I became convince of my place [or the lack of that] in it. I understood my fragility. I became obsess with preserving my beingness in this demoralizing milieu. I understood that I had to find a means to survive at all costs and by any method necessary. Just like my grandmother Vetto, I became a survivalist.

---

[6] I am referring to the person or the entity making a profit from someone else's pain and suffering.

BELIEVING IN GOD OR EXISTENTIALISM

I could not say that I do not believe in God. In truth, I believe in God. But my god is probably different from your own. I do not believe in God to the extent where I do not believe in myself. I am not an existentialist to the extent where I see myself as my own creator or my own divinity [or my own god].

What is the point in being an existentialist when one does not understand that one could not make oneself? Any person who denies God also denies the self, for God is the only reference men have for themselves. Other than that, men could only catch a glimpse of the self in the nothingness itself.

Existentialists are condemned to be selfless so long as they are godless. Existentialists could not have it both ways though. It is one way or another. That is, men need God or men need themselves. Put differently, it is either the case that men could renounce God or men could renounce themselves. But under no circumstance, men could be their own gods.

Men could not exist independently of their creator. To reiterate, the extent to which that creator is God is inconsequential. Whether that entity is something else [or someone else] is beside the point of this conversation.

Nonetheless, whether men could abandon God in a man's world is unclear. Even atheists need God to be themselves.

To be agnostic or not to believe in God or any divine power, for that matter, the person must first recognize the existence of a god. Of course, the individual would renounce the existence of that god or divinity for x or y reason. Thus, on the outset, every man believes in a God. Whether atheists believe in their belief to believe [or not to believe] is a different question, which is outside the realm of the present conversation.

Men exist in this world by evolving in an enduring paradox. They could not be unless they know the reason for their beingness. Nonetheless, the nature of a man's beingness eludes even the most brilliant thinkers in human history. Men have no clue about who they are. Thus, men could only speculate about their nature. God is the only proof men have of their existence.

Men could not know God unless they know themselves. In the same way, men could not renounce God unless they renounce themselves. There lies the tragedy of manhood. Men need to know the self before they could appreciate [genuinely of course] the insignificance of God for their own existence. So long as men want to be free, they could not be themselves, for their nature is intertwined with that of God.

A man could only know the self when he knows God. A man could only know God when he learns to uncover the self by referencing the divine. It is with great dismay that I proclaim that men could not be free so long as they exist on planet earth.

A man could not be free unless he could conceptualize what it means to know freedom outside the natural. Sadly, existentialism offers no substantial avenues for the man to uncover the self. Existentialism cannot teach the man about his nature. Existentialists have no clue about the nature of men. That is why existentialism needs God. The freedom that existentialists construe for men must come from God himself. From now, God is the original existentialist.

To be an existentialist is to become selfless. To be selfless is to be without God. To be without God is to be free. But to be free, at least as men envisage that state of being, is to be God. The problem is that such a state is unattainable.

The only way a man could be free [or to pretend to be that way] is for him to renounce God. But this aim, to say it again, is chimerical. Therefore, it is also unattainable. Men vacillate in the wilderness in the search of meaning. He constructs himself a place or a space, which he considers as a substitute for God or where such an entity might be. He calls it society. There, men were supposed to live in peace; they were supposed to live in harmony. This is a chimera.

Men epitomize their own venality. Their incapacity to grasp their own nature turns them into anti-humans. Men live in a constant quest for identity. But men are aware that God is the source of their identity. They understand that to renounce God is to renounce the self. From here, the freedom that men aspire outside the scope of God only exists in the nothingness. Beyond God, men know nothing about this world.

Without God, men have no purpose in this world. Without purpose, men could only linger in the nothingness. Without God, men are the nothingness.

This is the intellectual chasm, which existentialists have dug for themselves in trying to extirpate the man from his god, by it, giving the man his freedom, while depriving him of his god. This is a futile effort, for there could be no men without God. There could be no god without men.

The link between men and God is freedom or the lack of that. It is the dependence itself, which provides essence to a man's existence. Therefore, God is the provider of a man's essence or the sense of that. It is not the other way around.

Without considering God as the crux of the rationale for existence itself, existentialism would always be a failed intellectual project, for to be an existentialist is to be without God. The problem is that to be without God is to be deprived of a true sense of self. Tragically, for existentialists, existence always precedes essence. In the same manner, existentialism overlooks that essence [in and of itself] must come from God. Then, God must be the key to existence.

To say it otherwise, one cannot exist so long as one could not exist. The being could not be unless the being can be. For the being to be, he must have been before being in and of itself.

The spontaneity, which existentialist theorists presume that all men hold in their core beingness, must have had a point of departure. The being could not burst out of nowhere. If that were to be the case, then the being would have to have sprung from the nothingness itself. But that idea is repudiated vigorously by existentialism. Prominent existentialists, namely Sartre, have refuted that view.

BURSTING FROM THE NOTHINGNESS

To be in this world, the man must understand the need to be. The man must uncover why he exists. The man must grasp the reason he finds the self in this world and not in another. The man must grasp the reason for his existence.

The man must capture his *raison d'être*. He must become conscious of his own beingness. He must grasp the nature of the beingness, which others experience. The being [the man] could not provide essence to the self at a moment, which is before the self [itself], while identifying the nature of the self [itself]. The being could not be before he exists.

While I agree that the man could not know of his existence before he existed, he could not exist independently of his sense of self. He could not exist without grasping the need for that existence. To understand the reason for one's existence, the living being must have a point of reference. That point could be understood as the point of departure in the road to discovering the self. We could call that road a bridge to human essence. Existence needed not to preceding essence, for one is useless without the other. A man could not be [under any circumstance] before discovering the self. Existence and essence must exist in tandem.

The being could only uncover the self after the self has been revealed to him. The being could not situate the self before the self [itself] is situated. The being could not place the self in the world before the self [itself] is placed in that milieu. The being could not be before being *a priori*.

At no point before the being uncovers the self could he afford any sense of self to the self. The being could not provide essence to the self, for he did not know how to be. The being did not [or he could not] grasp what it means to be. The being did not grasp the nature of the self.

God is the only tangible path to which the being can [or could] uncover the self. In locating the self, the being becomes aware of the self. That reality affords the being the capacity to grasp the nature of his existence. In doing so, the being oversees the self. He provides essence to the self. The being finds God. It is not the other way around.

In the real world, existence comes after everything else. Human existence is a *de jour* reality, which has no tangible bearing [on its own]. The being could not impose his [own] existence in the face of that of others. This is the tragedy of human existence before the reality of the natural.

The selfless existence [or the Godless existence], which existentialists have proclaimed [or championed] over the years, is a pointless intellectual venture. To say it again, without God, there can be no self. Without the self, there is no need for existence. Without the need to exist, the being is akin to an object. The being could not uncover the self without uncovering God. He could not grasp the relevance of God without referencing the self. Without knowing God, the man would not need freedom, for he would have no use for it.

We could debate the nature of God [if God there is or if God could there be in the most tangible sense]. We could debate the role of God in helping men mitigate their problems. But this conversation is for another intellectual *tête-à-tête* about God, which is not for a near future.

NOT REFUTING GOD

I could not refute God in the present context. I could not refute existentialism either. Even though both ideals are incongruent, they have their utility for human survival. They are vital for the advancement of humanhood.

God is important in the life of a man. But accepting God must be sensible. I do not believe in faith-based beliefs, for they can be damaging for the believer. The person must be rational in his faith. Having faith alone is not enough to make a man fly in the sky like a bird, for the man was not designed to do so.

God is not indispensable. No matter what we do, we must find a way to substitute God in the absence of the divine, for without God, we would be selfless in a world where being empty of the self is a sure way of losing the self.

In substituting the divine, it would not be necessary to go to extraneous lengths. For convenience, we could call God's replacement *Mother Nature*. We could even claim that God does not exist. We could become existentialists.

We could call ourselves atheists, agnostics, or non-believers. We could even claim that we are not religious. We could say that we are spiritual.

We could claim that the secret of life lies in constant meditation. We could claim that life will reveal itself to us by evoking all sorts of absurd contrivances, which had been designed specifically to undermine the divine or even to highlight his presence in our lives. We could rely on the self [itself and by itself] to make it in this world. Whatever we do, we would have to have a god. If not, we could lose ourselves while searching for it.

I am not a disbeliever; I am not an existentialist. I could not see myself as a source of my own existence. That would be too pompous on my part. I did not make myself. I am a survivalist.

BEING A SURVIVALIST

I am a doubter. I am certain of nothing but my own doubt. I doubt everything in a man's world. I even doubt myself. My state of indistinctness also makes me wary of my existence, for I understand my fragility. I know that I have no power to change my reality.

My doubt is the source of my strength in my life. It is the engine of my resistance. My doubt provides me a sense of self in this perfidious milieu.

I have learned to rely on myself to outlive the malice that characterizes my brothers and sisters. I do not buy in the notion that human beings are righteous at their core. I have seen their evil nature firsthand. I have seen their pettiness in the vilest manner. I know they would resort to anything [or they would stoop] to any level to preserve their humanness. But they would do so to the damage of that of others. I have learned to do the same. That is why I am a survivalist.

Despite my faith in the divine, my existence could only be the result of my own efforts to exist by rights and not by chance. I have an intrinsic duty to persevere with myself and for my own self. I know that the world could become a cold and lonely place if I could not effort to surround myself with those who could help me preserve my beingness.

I know that men could easily go from predators to prey and vice versa. I must be conscious of the environment where I evolve. God has nothing to do with how I found the means to subsist. God does not determine the strategies I use to remain in a volatile milieu. I know that I am on my own, so I think. But God serves as a reference point in my life.

This is where I give existentialists credit in their appreciation [or the lack thereof] of the reality that men face during their dull existence. Under any conditions, the man must pay attention to his milieu. This is cardinal for him to survive beyond a lucky break. If believing in God helps the man become aware of his world, then he should embrace his God with all his strength. He should do so unconditionally.

If a man's ability to emancipate the self from the reality, which he faces, requires him to become a believer, so be it. If doing the same could be equated as a sign of freedom, then let the man be free to believe in God. That is why God and existentialism go together.

The freedom that might liberate a man from his troubles is the same freedom that might get him closer to God. But the closer the man gets to God, the more secluded he becomes. The only relevant substitute to either God or existentialism is the self itself.

So long as you believe in yourself, the sky would be the limit for your potential power to survive in this world beyond chance. God, or any divinity, for that matter, would become ornaments in your life. They could only help you give yourself a sense of self. But they could not protect you. They could not help you preserve your beingness in this treacherous world.

9

Good and Bad

Does the universe contain good and bad? There is a need to examine the nature of the man in an environment where good and bad interlock. Activities or conducts that could be made out [or even imagined] as *"good"* could also be considered as *"bad."* It depends on the circumstances in which a particular act is posed. It may depend on who finds the self in a situation of victimization because of the act itself.

Most people believe that every entity in the natural is beneath humanity. Some see themselves as a superior entity in nature. Many believe that they could seize anything in the world. They are the sole owners of the world and even themselves.

Despite the foolish nature of this view, it is the foundation on which the human world stands. Yes, this understanding of the way most people view the world, which others make out, implies ostentatiousness on my part. But it is not surreal. It is not the result of misguided assumptions about the world that others experience. Rather, it highlights erroneous ideals justifying the basis for human supremacy. It is a way of saying that there are real effects for holding [or even nurturing] such misguided understandings about the world. The world is not in black and white.

One of such mistaken approaches could be understood as the view that one man alone is responsible for his own misfortunes in this world. In no way is this understanding true. It must also be said that such a worldview is often echoed as a rationale or a tool to undermine human lives.

Within the human species, there is a stratified order, which awards certain groups with the capacity [or the ability] to set apart other humans. They often do so at will and with the evilest mindset. Men often display little to no sense of pity for their fellow men. In a social milieu, survival could be a dangerous undertaken. But the person experiencing the hard life often has no choice but to endure.

I would admit that life is not easy anywhere on planet earth. Life can be a horrendous experience for any living entity. This reality is even more demoralizing for the human species.

Men are battered, not by the natural, but simply for the fact of being men. Men know misfortune both in the natural and the artificial (a social milieu). By choice, this reality is more pronounced in a social setting.

There is no need to debate whether the world is pure or whether it could be sanctified. To reiterate, survival is guaranteed to no one in the natural. The same is true for the artificial milieu. This is so whether the man finds the self in nature or in a social milieu. No matter what, the man must find his way. He must do so on his own and for his own.

A SANCTIFIED WORLD

There is no way to come up with an objective assessment of a sanctified milieu. We could not envisage a world where every entity lives in peace [or in harmony]. This would go against the fundamentals of the natural milieu itself.

The notion that there could be peace in the natural space could be described as a misguided view about the reality of the world. The natural landscape could never have peace. This is an exogenous idea, which could not explain the reality that pervades in the natural milieu. Peace, at least as now understood, could only benefit the weak to the harm of the strong.

Amid the chaos, which is nature itself, there is a clear structure; there is a distinct order. Every being is strong in the natural. There, the man is subjected to the reality of the environment. The man's mastery of the place would determine whether he has the capacity to resist the milieu.

Nature does not reward weakness. This place depends on the strong to guarantee its existence. The weak would hasten the unavoidable destruction of the natural. But the weak could not prevail in the natural, although such entities might thrive within the social space.[7]

There is no peace in the natural. There could not be such a happening. Peace would symbolize the death of nature. But there would be no one to witness that peace. There would be nothing to which peace would matter. There

---

[7] When I speak of being weak, I am referring to entities that might be incapable of defending themselves.

would be no nature. It would be the *"Nothingness"* (*Le Néant*). With good grace, if that were to be the case, we would not be able to recognize the nothingness itself, if it were to occur. We would simply not *"be."* We could not appreciate what *"not being"* would look like or would feel like.

The idea that there is a world out there where *"everything can be"* harmoniously or fine and dandy is a testament of our unfamiliarity of the den where we live in. This reality also suggests our gullible nature. There is only one life. It is the life of now.

There is *"you"* and there is *"the world."* Everything might be on your shoulder. Everyone [or everything in this world] might be against you. In any case, you must preserve your beingness by any means necessary. You must hustle. You must survive. You must carry on. Beyond that point, there is nothing else to scramble for in the world. It is the man against the world; it is the world against the man.

The previous understanding is important to grasp. This is where existentialism, to echo, is useful in making it possible for men to grasp the link between existentialist ideals and God. This is also where God plays a crucial role in helping men preserve their beingness. As it were, this is where existentialism and dogma intersect. Therefore, I would argue here as well, it is crucial for men to understand their reality with a practical lens.

Everything wants to capture the man. But the man must do all he can to bide in a man's world. Life often becomes a struggle, which the man could never experience in its fullest.

The man is a mortal. He could not supersede his nature. He could not overlook his essence or the lack of that. Fewer men could grasp their fragility, even though most men understand that they could not overcome their reality. The man would also claim ownership of his beingness. He would boast his made-out control over the natural. That control would be tangible only for other men. A man's hubris comes from his obliviousness or his egotism.

In the real world, there is no *after* life. The man must go all out to remain alive. He must do so today; he must do so tomorrow. Like this, the man must fall over backwards to ride out until the end.

Nature has no favorite. In that space, everyone must perish as a condition to further the continuity of the natural milieu. It is either you eat some or you are eaten by some. There is no mitigation to that depressing truth.

Despite it all, the man must hold on in the natural. He must do so above all. The man must be. Let the man be, at least, for the being' sake!

FAITH AND RELIGION

Before we delve in this part of the conversation, let me echo that the previous assertions were not brewed to undermine those who hold religious views. My theory about God is not an affront to faith or religion. In making these concessions, this is not an effort on my part to be apologetic for the views inscribed throughout this manuscript so far.

Let me point out that we could not relate the nature of the man without mentioning their spiritual strength. God may be a source of strength for the being. Believing in something or in someone could provide the man a reason to carry on during his calamities.

While God might be important for human survival, he is not indispensable. Many people have found their way in this world without God. Every man has his own god. But that reality does not mean that God does not exist or could not exist. Knowing God is a personal effort. The man must understand that actuality for his own sake.

I could not be a religious skeptic. That does not mean that I am certain that there is [in fact] a god. I do not know that for sure. Regardless, I consider myself a man of faith.[8]

---

[8] I was brought up in a Christian environment. For a good portion of my life, I have always gone to church. When I became an immigrant, I found

Despite my made-out insights about the world, I am certain of nothing in that milieu. I do not know whether I need a god or not. Considering the atrocities that mark this world, I doubt that there is a god who oversees everything and everyone. God is inconsequential in the world, which men experience in their mundane.

After saying all that, I must point out that I have no qualm against God. I have no reason to refute God's existence. I also have no reason to claim [at least with certainty] that there is a god. I doubt my own doubt about God.

When it comes to God, I am certain of my misgivings. That is also the strength of my beliefs; it is the source of my own strength, for I am aware of my own fragility in a world where my only recourse is my capacity to recognize that I have none.

While I could not deny the divine, I could not undermine God's conceivable power to guide men in their crucibles in life. Then again, I am uncertain that God could make the man whole. I am not sure that God could spare the man from his nature. I could not see the man as a superhuman in a milieu where everything was designed to tear men apart.

---

it difficult to continue that practice. There is a business facet to religion in America. I refuse to be a part of it.

Likewise, I could not undermine God's role in a man's life. I could not minimize the role that God may play in my own living experience. Notwithstanding my awareness of my world, God [or his absence] is a source of my strength in it.

God is important for my existence. God may help me navigate my realities [be they social or else], at least spiritually. I am also aware that God may not be able to help me beyond my own capacity to help myself. God may be powerless in the face of the calamities, which other men brought about in my life.

I am convinced that believing in God is a good strategy for survival. That belief could help you prolong your existence in this treacherous world. You would not want to be left stranded on the heels of heaven's doors [if heavens doors there are] because you doubted the power of God.

I could not say that there is no god. I have no reason to feel that way, for I am not an anti-God. Absolutely, I believe in the existence of a higher power. I am also aware that such a power might not be as omnipotent in my social life as I would like it to be. That power might not be as omnipresent in my world as I would like it to be. The previous concerns are not enough to undermine that power.

FINDING GOD'S IDENTITY

Where could we find God? Is God in the sky? Is God anywhere but the sky? I am not sure how to answer these questions. Here, I could not give you a hint of an answer.

I am not sure of God's identity. I am not sure whether God is Allah, Buddha, Jehovah, Krishna, Shakti, Shiva, Vishnu, Legba, Papa Hogou, or Yahweh, to name a few. Still, I am certain that humanity is not empty of an overseer. I am not without an overseer. This is the source of my strength in my milieu. This is what keeps me going in it.

Regardless of the previous allocutions, little is clear about the existence of God beyond faith. Who is God then? To what degree that God is as powerful as many people believe him to be? I do not know. But it is unlikely that anyone has a clear answer.

Most people want to share God with the rest of the world. But do they really have God? Perhaps not.

You could not give to others what you do not have. You could not point out to others what you do not see. God is that elusive gift, which most people want to give away when they do not even have it themselves. Nobody owns God.

If any human being had access to God, every human being would have a similar access. There would be no need to be enlightened by someone other than oneself. Despite views to the contrary, God [if God there is or if God there were] is not exclusive, where only a few [chosen individuals] have access to him.

God is the being—whom some say reign supreme. Most people pretend to see and feel God. Is that the case?

Some people say that God has spoken to them. As a result, they enjoy a special connection with the Almighty. But no one can point God out, even in the void of the sky. No one knows who God is; no one knows where God is. Yet, most people want to give God away to those that they think deserve God the most.

Can you see [or can you sense] the absurdism of the previous understandings? I hope that you could do so, for doing so would help you find your way in this world. Then again, this milieu is filled with bad faith individuals. They are out to pledge their own existence by undermining yours.

I prefer to appraise the world on my own and for my own. I ponder about the world. I reflect on my reality in that milieu. I ponder on the circumstances, which others may experience. I am attuned to my conditions. I appraise the entities that make up my surroundings. I cherish the entities that set up my reality, whether they are good or bad [or whether they could be either way]. I make myself no illusion about their true intents to undermine my own. I do not rely on others to show me what is inside me. I do not rely on others to further my own existence. I could do it independently. This is not just my reality.

The man has the natural capacity to discover the world for himself. Adhering to someone else's profession of the world might induce the person to develop a misguided understanding about nature. This might affect that person's understanding of life itself. The man must find his way to the world. He must do so by himself and for himself.

RELYING ON GOD

I do not subject myself to the Gods of the Godless people of my milieu. I prefer to believe that there is something akin to God in the megacosm. That something could also be the natural.

If there were a *God,* he would be everywhere. God would be available to everyone [or to anyone]. The same God would protect both the hunter and the hunted.

When you catch a chicken and take possession of its beingness to prolong your own, could we say that God blessed both you and the chicken? You might say that you received blessings from God because he gave you the opportunity to eat the chicken. You might also say that the chicken enjoys God's blessings by helping you further your own existence. We could say that God gave the chicken the opportunity to be eaten by you solely to further the continuity of the natural milieu itself.

This view about human existence might seem unorthodox. Some might even consider it strange. Indeed, this approach is not in line with traditionally held beliefs about the role of God in a man's world. It does not jibe with the relevance of human beings within the natural. In fact, the common supposition is that humans own the world. They do so by rights. They are blessed in the universe. But they are certain that only they [that is, humans] enjoy such a rapport with the *Almighty*.

The previous consideration brings up an interesting question. How could a person be blessed for leaving four fawns in the forest to starve to death after he took their mother away from them? How could a person be blessed when he killed another or when he seized the beingness of another? He did not do it for survival. He did it because he could do so.

From a societal lens, we could ask similar questions. For instance, what makes you rich and what makes other individuals poor? What justify your lavish lifestyle in the face of my abjectness? Why are you? Why I am not? Why, why, why?

I know; you would spew the usual nonsense to justify your pettiness. You would say that God blessed you. To that I would say, too bad I am not the chosen one. Too bad! Indeed, too bad for me. Why am I a sacrilege? Why you and not me? Better yet, why me and not you? I do not have any answer.

Notwithstanding your wonderful fate, as opposed to my sordid reality, you are not better than me. You are not better than anyone. You are just another man.

My point is that it is unfair that you get to be while I only get to watch you being. It is unfair to struggle to be, while your beingness is handed down to you. God has nothing to do with your good fortunes; that is, if "good fortunes" we could call your reality. God has nothing to do with my putrid fate.

Then again, I must ask, why such an extravagant life? Why you deserve it all and I, none? You are a mortal, just like the rest of us. You do not need more than a loath of bread to survive. Why do you deny the same to me and others like me?

Okay, for the sake of the argument, let us say that God chose you. Why would God [if God there were] reward you after you have already rewarded yourself by taking the life of another as your prize? What God would that be? Tell me, for I am missing something about the world.

Maybe I am blinded by my own biases. What is plain is that I could not grasp the reality of nature. It is likely that I am too narrow-minded. I could not capture the world, which most people have mastered through prayer or through their connection with God. Then again, how could there be a God when there is so much pain and misery? I do not get it. Please, men of God, enlighten me, if you could.

PART IV

Life is Right Now

10

Existing in the Moment

Life is now. Living, as existentialists would claim, is in the moment; it is not tomorrow. I would go even further. I would say that living is to remain on planet earth; it is not to be on Mars or anywhere else.

The man must embrace his nature within the natural. Human beings must make the best of their existence. They must thrive in the milieu where they find the self.

As a species, we must be. We must prosper. We must be all that we could be, be it in the natural or in the artificial. While this view could be considered peripheral in the real world, it is not in error. It is an inquisitive approach to the reality of the world, which men face in their quotidian.

For most people, there is no link between God and the natural. God stands alone (or God is on his own). The Almighty God, they say, is a Supreme Being. The great creator, God [they also say] guides human beings on earth.

For others, nature is an incidence in a man's world. It is an indescribable, usually an annoying, milieu or an entity, which burdens human lives. The natural milieu, some are convinced, is antithetic to human nature.

Many people consider nature an impediment for human progress. But few people know where to find nature. Fewer people could realize their role in the natural milieu. A much smaller group could grasp the significance of the natural.

The theory is that nature is an exogenous place. It must be sought; it must be preserved; it must be cherished. But this is ludicrous.

There is the view that nature could be lethal for human survival. I cannot grasp the rationale for such an axiom. The real world is different from the actuality, which a person may make out about his reality.

The pervading belief is that there is a need to go out and explore nature. Many people believe that there is a need to avoid nature. What an absurdity.

I would admit that deciphering nature can be akin to resolving a paradox. The natural contained entities, which could affect the man in the most negative ways. The woods, the forests, or the jungle could become deathtraps. They could become places of misery.

The reality of nature, many people believe, is dangerous for humans [or for the species]. This view is based on the notion that nature is different from anything else. This view is also inaccurate.

SOCIETY VERSUS NATURE

To what degree society is different from nature? We could approach this question from many angles. For conciseness, let us say that there would be no society without nature.

The belief is that nature and society are two different entities. Nature is within the forest or it is within the wilderness, they say. Nature is far away from civilizations, some are certain.

Society, according to popular beliefs, is located where humans live. The view is that a social milieu is a safer environment for the human species to thrive; at least, some are convinced that this is always the case.

As an alternative to the natural, society is the platform on which the human species could thrive. The person has a better chance for survival within a social setting, they say. I disagree. I would say that only the opposite is true.

People forget that humans have every possible means at their disposal to make it within the natural. We are wild beings. There is nothing wrong in finding ourselves in the natural. There is nothing wrong in being in the wilderness. Our destiny was not to live in cage-like settings, whether it be psychological or mental (social rules) or whether it be physical or emotional (prisons or jails). Humans were not designed to experience artificially induced constraints.

Contrary to popular misconceptions, the natural is not a trap. Nature is not a prison for the being. While humans are bounded on the planet, we have the potential to explore the natural in its most elementary state. We have no restrictions in our ability to be in nature. There, we have fewer limits. But we have the discretion of exploring the natural milieu to the degree that nature would allow it.

Considering our unrestricted access to the natural, we have been to places. We have imagined places. We have construed others. In the natural, we are no prisoners; at least, this is not the case in the true sense of being confined in a physical cage.

There are no other livable places where men could have no end. Apart from planet earth, we have no place to go. This is our home. This is where we belong. Yet, we do not know this milieu well enough.

There are places on planet earth where we have never visited. Somehow, we long to go to Mars. We long to conquer other planets. We see ourselves as mini gods. Is this not absurd?

WHERE WE BELONG

The reality of the humankind is that we could not evolve anywhere but on planet earth. We could not do so on a long-term basis. On earth, the natural does not restrict us. Nothing in that milieu could stop us from venturing in places, which are inhospitable. This is the beauty of being in the natural.

Even though humans were not designed to live in space, we have been there. We have seen the wonders of the natural. Somehow, we are convinced that we could tame the natural milieu itself. Human beings have shown capacities, which no other living beings have proved so far.

We regularly visit space. We have modeled magnificent gadgets. We have built wonderful structures. To the casual observer, we are as grandiose as God could ever be. But that, in and of itself, does not make us gods; at least, not in the true sense of the word "Divinity."

Human beings could not fly on their [own] volition. Granted, we have found the means to experience flight. We have found ways to be both under and over the water. We have built submarines; we have built boats and other vessels. Still, these achievements are a sign that nature is not restrictive. While the natural limits the man, it does not restrict him.

Being in society is a different reality. This milieu is inherently restrictive. There, the man could not be unless he has been allowed to be. Most people could not cope with the reality of being confined in a social milieu. They find themselves in a constant struggle to tame their [own] selves before someone else does it. Life becomes a heartbreak. Nothing outside the natural is a normal instance.

Society eats men. Nature, on the other hand, breeds them. This is a poignant difference, which no man should undermine.

What might explain the reason humans make their existence so precarious? What might explain the reason that we evolve in such comedic arrangements? I do not have any answers. But it is irrefutable that we know nothing about ourselves.

FACING OUR HUBRIS

Why do humans suffer so much in this world? I do not know. Of course, I am not the only one who has no clue.

Why does the previous understanding elude most thinkers? A reasonable explanation is *obliviousness.* I could refer to our *hubris* to explain that reality.

We know so little about ourselves that we are willing to accept anything about our reality, which seems convincing enough. We are dazzled before the immensity of the universe, which we are yet to uncover in its full extent. We are *gaga* before the natural state of nature. We think that the stars are pretty. We are certain that the flowers are beautiful. We are definite that the forest is breathtaking. It is as if these entities were designed to be aesthetically pleasing to men.

We seldom recognize our reality in the natural in its fullest. We overlook that an eternal conflict for survival is brewing underneath the obvious beauty, which we make out in the natural. We imagine a world of harmony when the natural is never in synchrony.

The world is far from knowing any sense of unity. We live in a world in disarray. This is also the reality, which characterizes the world that men experience. Only, they seldom admit it.

The world is far from being a place of harmony. It is far from experiencing peace. The agitations that characterize the milieu make the world what it is.

Underneath the seeming tranquility and the sense peace, which we make out about the world, a well-orchestrated violence is underway. A savagery is taking place everywhere on the planet. This is the nature of the world. However, most of us could only sense that reality.

Human beings could do nothing to stop the natural. Nature did not give us the capacity to reverse it. If there were a supreme truth, this would be it. This is the nature of the natural. We could never undermine it. We could only witness its wonders and its splendor.

We are flabbergasted before the magnificence of planet earth. We are astonished before the vast nature of the ocean. We are lost in the multiplicity of the creatures that roam through the planet. We are confused about why the earth shakes. We are irresolute about the reason the earth burns. We do not grasp the reason the ocean immerses us. We do not grasp why the water, which our existence depends on, drowns us.

We find ourselves lost in the world. We do not grasp why other living entities seek to overpower us. We could not realize why earth-born or air-born creatures want to consume us. We are confused about the reality of our life. Sadly, that sense of haughtiness iɳ men is the foundation of existentialist philosophy.

11

Being is Essential

Men often become caught up in their arrogance. Men think they are supposed to be above anything else in the natural. They think that they have a right to be here. Men feel that they are entitled to be. Before the reality of their blemishes and failings, they appeal to divinities.

Men imagine a world where life could be without being. They dream of a life after life. They hope to live forever in the heavens. This is not the case in any way, shape, or form.

Men dream of immortality. Some of them think that God is the key. Some men believe that the divine is going to make it possible for them to unlocking their true potentials. They think that God is the answer to their thrift. They seldom admit that they do not have a hunch about the realities that lay bare right before their eyes.

For many existentialist theorists, there is no god. They think that there is something else to exert the self for in life. They think that there is another side to life, which is better.

No one knows of the existence of any alternative to their current living arrangements other than the reality that they are experiencing daily. They think that there is something out there. This is not that way in any way, shape, or form.

Life is now. It is right on. It is nowhere else. Life will not supervene in the future; at least, it will not be in that way glaringly. Life is taking place right now.

Men must embrace life with all their vigor. They must live today. They should not preserve the life of today, for another day, for tomorrow belongs to nature. They must look forward to tomorrow only to improve their lives in the natural. They must do so right now.

Men must understand that they are not nature. Men must realize that they could not be the natural. Men are simply a part of the natural.

LET THE "BEING" BE

Why humans construe a world for themselves beyond the world that nature affords them? Is it because they can think? Is it because they can reflect on the world beyond its actual characteristics? I am not sure how to answer.

Despite the previous revelations, there are no clear answers about the world. The nature of this milieu is a mystery to the human mind. Despite our views about the world, we know nothing about ourselves in it. We know nothing about the world itself.

The notion that God is omnipotent is misguided. The view that there is a life-after-life is in error. To reiterate a previous assertion, living is now. Seeing the world otherwise could lead to our premature downfall.

Nothing in the tangible suggests that men could exist in another dimension. Nothing in the natural suggests such a possibility. It is not clear whether men could transcend to a state of consciousness after death. Seeing the world from such an angle could be a sign of our incapacity to grasp our reality. It could be a sign of our ignorance about ourselves. It could be the figment of our wildest imagination.

Regardless of how men may make out their actuality, a clear veracity hinders their beingness. The man must be in tuned with that reality. The man must be authentic. He must remain in the real world. He should not be in the surreal. The man must [first] *be* in the *real world* before he could be in the *dreamlike world*.

When I say, *"Preserving your beingness,"* that does not mean that you should stop being in the real world. That does not mean that you should defer yourself to a world of fantasy or a milieu laden with imaginary possibilities, which would never become concrete in the real world. Instead, you must be aware of yourself. You must accept the reality of your beingness in that milieu.

There is no doubt about it; the real world can be lethal. Every being in that space must be aware of that reality. We were designed to be in this world. We were not designed to be on the Moon or on Mars. We were not designed to live underwater. We were designed to live on planet earth.

The man must be on earth. He belongs in this milieu. Anything else would be the product of our imagination. You should not become a lion's dinner because of bad karma. You should be attuned to lions or other beings, many of whom mull around you. Nonetheless, many of them might be disguised as men like you.

You should not lose your beingness because you did not envisage the possibility that you might lose it to further the natural. You should know the self. You should not overlook the likelihood of losing yourself. You must be aware of the dangerous nature of being in the natural. That knowledge could help you adjust yourself.

Many of us are not aware of the world that we experience. Even when the world is obvious before our eyes, we might be prone to overlook its intricacies. We think that we could be in the natural without being an element of nature. But this is a gullible way of concretizing our reality. Thinking that we could tame the natural is outlandish.

We create our own hope out of the thin air. We overlook the life that is passing right before our eyes. We look to a life that we could only live theoretically, in abstract, or in the *quantum* world. But that life is an illusion. It only exists, so long as we can imagine it. That life is the product of our mind's eye. It is not real; it could never be that way.

ACCEPTING OUR REALITY

Men must accept their truth in this world. The problem is that men often overlook that they are in the present. Men often ignore that they are part of the beingness itself.

Whether the creator of that world [or the architect of the man or the being itself] is God, or whether we could refer to that entity as nature, is inconsequential. What is relevant is that we are in the present. We must continue to be in it. We must embrace our reality in that actuality.

We may never know (at least for a fact) whether God exists. Nonetheless, we would always know our [own] existence, for we have the potential to become conscious of the self. We must be aware of our awareness. That alone is proof of our existence.

If we could ponder, we could accept our reality for what it is and not how it is presented to us. Although we might not be certain of that reality, we would always know that there is nothing else to uncover in the world. This is the essence of our life. This is the essence of our beingness.

As René Descartes put it, *Cogito, ergo sum.* To put it another way, *I think, therefore I am.* Doubt gives the man the capacity to know the self or to discover the self around others. When you doubt, you accept the infinite possibility of being someway or somewhere. No divinity could replace that, although God could help you accept that truth.

Certain facets about the world might never be learned by men. Deducing life in its fullest is not possible; at least, this is not the case at the level that we are experiencing the world. If there were any reality [or any actuality] significant beyond this world, it would be the nothingness itself. Anything beyond the world that we experience would be inconsequential for our beingness. It would not be for us, as human beings, to know or to even to postulate.

We belong on *terra firma*. The world is ours. Life is occurring right here. It is happening right now. We would be better off embracing that life the way that it presents itself to us.

We should experience life while it is flowing before our eyes. We have one life to live; it is in the present. We must accept that fact.

BEING LOST IN THE WORLD

Many of us have found ourselves looking for our way out of the natural. We may feel lost. We could not tap into the *self-within-the-self*. Making sense of our reality in a man's world may make no sense at all. We must gravitate toward God.

Relying on a divinity or a higher power makes no more sense than making sense of our own realities. Denying nature does not mean that nature no longer controls us. It does not mean that nature no longer governs our relationship with the world.

We should know that God could not stop a lion from consuming us. But we should not deceive ourselves. We should not justify our obliviousness by evoking our faith. Existentialists would call that reality *Mauvaise Foi* or *Bad*

Faith.[9] We nourish the idea that God would not put us on the path of a lion. I doubt that God is aware of the [supposed] choices that we make, or the ones that are made on our behalf.[10]

If God could direct us whenever and wherever he pleases, then we would have no sense of ourselves. We would be akin to robots. We would not be free. We could not be that way under any circumstances.

If men were under the reach of God, at least, the divine as now understood, we would not be independent thinkers. We could not even think of such likelihood. We would not be dimensional beings. We would be just an instance in the natural.

While I would not say that we are free to the extent that we make our destiny, I would concede that we have a control over our realities. That control is conditioned to our

---

[9] The concept of *bad faith* was advanced by Jean-Paul Sartre in his attempt to help make sense of human ontology. The term bad faith implies the notion of a physical manifestation of a person's intransigence.

[10] The notion of choice is more complicated than the way I denote it throughout the text. I am not convinced that human beings have real choices. I debate this issue in another publication. Please refer to *Crime and Nature* to learn more.

ability to recognize our reality. Claiming that we are free as a result is far-fetched.

In every fiber of our being, we know that we are not free. This could never be the case under any circumstances. Despite it all, we know that we are not automated beings. We know that we are a part of the natural. What we do or what we omit from doing is natural. We are a part of a whole, although we have our own identity in it. That does not mean that we are always free to be however [or whenever] that we might please to be.

FREE FROM OURSELVES

Are human beings free in the world? I would say not at all. At a fundamental level, I must admit it here, something in the cosmos guides us through our journey in the world. Even though we may perceive ourselves to be free, we also know that we are constrained.

The "supposed" freedom, which we enjoy in the natural, is limited. This understanding is based on our feeble capacity to grasp that reality. And so, we enjoy little [if any] freedom outside the natural, which may explain why our social reality can be so demoralizing.

As I have tried to explain throughout this diatribe, life in a social milieu can be ingenuously miserable. We must reckon that this reality is inescapable. We are in a social contract, which we did not bargain with [or we did not ask for it]. We are the slaves of our milieu. So long as we could not see that reality, we would suffer in that milieu.

We have no choice; we must apply ourselves to outlive our troubles. We must strive to remain whole, though we would do so in futility. The fight for survival is infinite.

We were put together so we could be in this world. We are human beings. No other planet could save us from our natural calamities. So long as we think that we hold an ownership claim over our own selves, we are condemned to remain in an eternal state of bondage. We must recognize that there is no escape. We are doomed to live on planet earth. We are condemned to be here.

Although we may think that we enjoy freedom, we know that we are not like that; we know that we could never be free. Yet, we rationalize our freedom. We justify any sense of that self-determination to ourselves. We roam the earth in the search of a place to exist by claim and not by rights.

We refuse to allow ourselves to be. It is important that we consider the degree to which being in the world irrevocably demands us to be free from our own dominions. We must free ourselves from ourselves. This is the essentiality of being in the world.

12

Refuting God in the World

Many people are without guidance; they may feel lost in their world. From their vantage point, God is different from the natural. Some people are convinced that human beings are distinct from the natural as well. It is as if humans were the direct descendants of God.

The presumption is that humans are God-like in their [own] nature. In most atheist circles, the belief is that human beings are God. If not, they have God-like traits.

This is absurd; this is intellectual rubbish. If not, this view is, in its most harmless sense, snobbish. It is, to say the least, pretentious; it is egotistical. It is even dangerous to see ourselves from such a prism.

I often ask myself whether those who view the world from such an angle are aware of the cosmos. Have they realized that there is more humanity in us that our hubris could fathom? There is more to existence than claiming control over the wonderful nature of planet earth.

Are they aware of their place in the universe? Are they aware of the insignificance of the human species in that milieu? How could they think that humanity is the best thing that happened to the universe? How could this be?

Another fringe of people believes that life culminates by finding God. But God, I must accept it here, is the Almighty. Even if there were a God, no one would know where that God is. No one would know where he might be. No one would know who that God is [or who he might be]. No one could tell anyone where to find that God.

There is a reality out there. Once the man has been sprung into this world, the struggle to stay there is his. The man must find a way to comfort himself against the elements. God [if God there is or if God there could be] that entity would have little or nothing to do with the reality, which the man confronts in the real world.

The man meanders in nature in the search of allies. But he does so in the hope of prolonging his existence. The fact remains that the man is left to fend for the self.

The man is alone anywhere that he finds the self. He must grasp his fortune or the lack of that. He must navigate the milieu where he finds the self. The man must learn to deal with his ups and downs, be they artificially imposed or naturally induced.

The man must learn to be in this world. He must learn to do so without the protectorate of a god or any other entities. The man must rely on the self to prolong his beingness. Doing so could be supreme for the man to guarantee his survival in a space, which has been designed to make his existence dangerous.

The man must master the elusiveness of his beingness. He must realize that men might be the cause of his miseries. He must rely on neither faith no fate to survive.

LIVING IN A MAN'S WORLD

We are on earth. This place has transmuted over the years. It has been transformed into a lethal milieu for mankind.

Sadly, that transformation is the result of men's inability to understand themselves in the world where they evolve.

Overtime, the earth has been turned into a nightmare for the human species. It is a man's world now. This is not God's kingdom; that is, if it ever were that way.

If God were to be out there (in the sky) or in here (in your heart), he/she/it would be an important ally to have in the battle fields of life. God could help you win the war of survival. You would need to embrace anything that might lead you closer to that god. This approach to your existence would be the best way to prolong your survival in this treacherous world.

I do not take the world (both the social place and the natural space) for granted. I do not underestimate my relevance there or the lack of that. I am conscious of my place in the macrocosm. I am inclined to think of the places that others hold in this world. I understand that the failure to do so could lead to my premature death. That is why I say that a person must preserve his beingness at all costs and under any circumstances. But to do so, the individual must become aware of the self. He must philosophize.

Despite the earlier assertions, I could never be certain of whom [or what] I am in the world. I could never be firm about whom or what guards me. I do not know the purpose of my presence on this earth.

I am here. I must make the best of my presence on this magnificent place called earth. But I am not sure for what purpose some entity would protect me.

I know that because of my lack of certainty about who is watching the world, whether from above, from within, or from below, I am inclined to believe in the power that the tangible forces, which guide this world, might have over me. That force is nature. The natural and God are the same. If not, they are interconnected.

NATURE VERSUS GOD

The world is governed by natural forces. Such forces provide a blanket of safety and security to all living entities, including humans through their journey. Nature is a power source; this milieu guides human beings through their crucibles.

We could call nature the god of all gods. We could refer to the natural as a portal to God. We could not remove the natural from God. We could not ignore the role of God in the natural.

It is likely that God [if God there is or if God there could be] intertwines with nature. The natural could be a pedestal for God. The natural milieu could be the medium on which god exists. This would be the case, even if God were to exist in this world or in any other worlds. This would be that way if we lived in theory [or in the immaterial]. It would be that way if we lived in the supernatural sense [that is, the invisible].

God would be nature or nature would be God in disguise. As a result, any human being could tap into the power of the natural. He could do so as if he had been communicating with God himself. This would help the man further his beingness. Everything in the universe is God's creation or it is God's design. This is a claim, which few men of faith could refute.

We could say that both God and nature are diametrically different. But what would that mean for the man? Would this mean that the man is left to fend for himself in the wilderness? I would say no.

We could also claim that God and nature are similar. Would that mean that God is responsible for both the good and the bad, which the person experiences in the world? I would say yes. That would also mean there is something in the natural aura that tenders to the being.

If there were no god [or if there were no gods] anywhere in the universe, would this mean that the man would be without any guidance? This would be unlikely, I say. The man would still have nature.

Unlike God, there is no misgiving about where nature is located. The natural, to reiterate, is everywhere. The man is always in contact with that nature. Unquestionably, the degree to which he is aware of that back and forth remains unclear. But the man must find nature. He must place himself in that milieu.

ACCESSING THE NATURAL

Some people might find it difficult to accept that nature is part of their nature. The only portal available for men to communicate with the natural is easily accessible. The man can find nature through his capacity to reflect on his reality.

Nature is not a mystery. Every being can absorb the events that are occurring in the natural. Through that absorption, the man could see the world from a natural dimension. Such a dimensional angle would allow the man to foresee important moments in his life. These moments could entangle the man's own existence.

A being or a person who is in tuned with nature is also harmonious with time. The man could anticipate events and other happenings within the scenery where he settles in. The man would be in the best position to preserve his relevance, however small or however insignificant it might be, within the natural. The man would be a whole with nature.

Being in tuned with nature could offer the man the capacity to merge with the natural. The man could be unencumbered. He could free the self from unnecessary loads and meaningless obstacles to outwear his milieu. The man would be on top of the world.

Nature offers the man a glimpse into the real world. But the man often ignores nature. From here, there is a need to rethink our rapport with the natural. Philosophy gives the man an unlimited access into the natural world. The man must become aware of the self within the natural space.

Philosophy gives the man an edge over other beings. When the man relates to his nature, he might view the world as is. The man might predict events, which might be detrimental to his beingness. The man would be able to foresee situations, which could hurt his ability to wear well in the world.

In being in constant contact with the natural, the man would be in total control over the self. He would master the extent to which other beings could affect his beingness. The man would be beyond serendipity. In any case, the man would be for his own sake; that is, however ephemeral such a state of being might be.

Final Words

BEING IN THE WORLD is not complicated. However, the man must learn to recognize situations, which could be lethal to his beingness. The man must be in tuned with the world. To achieve that aim, I would say, the man must philosophize.

There is a need for a better understanding of the natural. There is also a need for the man to recognize the role that spirituality might play in helping the man preserve his beingness. Life can be a chimerical undertaken. Despite everything, the degree to which society could be harmful to human beings is not well understood.

Living in society is a *de facto reality.* Human beings must be attuned to this milieu. They must adjust themselves to that actuality. They must do so synchronically.

Philosophy and life intertwine. The man must be attuned to the world (both inside and out). This is the best way for him to make sense of his crucibles.

The man must ponder. This is quintessential for him to carry through. Philosophy becomes a great way for the man to reflect on both the self and other entities within the space where he evolves.

The nature of *human ontology* could be difficult to disentangle. There is not enough data in the literature to help us decipher the nature of the man. Even so, the extent to which human beings are the only entity could produce thoughts at the most introspective level is also unsettled. In it lies the crux of the issues, which I sought to highlight here.

We must philosophize to persist in this world beyond fortuity. We must preserve our beingness within the natural. We are condemned to evolve in this milieu. We must be regardless of the impediments or the obstacles that might take away our beingness.

Every being must be. Every being can be. Every being should be. This has been my motto for a long time. I think. I philosophize. I strategize. So, *Cogito, Ergo Philosophus,* for I am in the world of men. I am the only divinity in my own world. I am my own god in a man's world, for I believe in myself more than I do in anything [or in anyone] else…

Index

About the Author

BEN WOOD JOHNSON, Ph.D.

Dr. Johnson is a social observer, a philosopher, and a multidisciplinary scholar. He writes about law, legal theory, education, public policy, politics, race and crime, and ethics.

Dr. Johnson graduated from Penn State University and Villanova University. He holds a Doctorate in Educational Leadership, a Master's degree in Political Science, a Master's degree in Public Administration, and a Bachelor's degree in Criminal Justice.

Dr. Johnson worked in law enforcement. He attended John Jay College of Criminal Justice. Dr. Johnson is fluent in several languages, including French, Spanish, Portuguese, and Italian.

Dr. Johnson enjoys reading, poetry, painting, and music. You may contact Dr. Ben Wood Johnson by e-mail or via postal services. See other information below.

Mailing Address

Eduka Solutions
330 W. Main St, #214
Middletown, PA 17057

E-mail

E-mail Address: tkpubhouse@gmail.com

Social Media

Find Dr. Ben Wood Johnson on the following media platforms.

Twitter: @benwoodpost
Facebook: @benwoodpost

You may find Dr. Ben Wood Johnson on other online platforms, including his official blog site at www.benwoodpost.org. You may visit his website at www.benwoodjohnson.com. If you would like to learn more about Dr. Johnson's works, you may find them on his official bookstore at www.benwoodjbooks.com.

Other Works

Selected works by Dr. Ben Wood Johnson

1. Racism: What is it?

2. Sartrean Ethics: A Defense of Jean-Paul Sartre as a Moral Philosopher

3. Jean-Paul Sartre and Morality: A Legacy Under Attack

4. Sartre Lives On

5. Forced Out of Vietnam: A Policy Analysis of the Fall of Saigon

6. Natural Law: Morality and Obedience

7. Cogito Ergo Philosophus

8. Le Racisme et le Socialisme: La Discrimination Raciale dans un Milieu Capitaliste

9. International Law: The Rise of Russia as a Global Threat

10. Citizen Obedience: The Nature of Legal Obligation

TESKO PUBLISHING

www.teskopublishing.com

www.ingramcontent.com/pod-product-compliance
Lightning Source LLC
Chambersburg PA
CBHW022024090426
42739CB00006BA/279

9 781948 600354